D1521526

RAFTS
& Other
RIVERCRAFT
in *Huckleberry Finn*

RAFTS
& Other
RIVERCRAFT
in *Huckleberry Finn*

Peter G. Beidler

UNIVERSITY OF MISSOURI PRESS
Columbia

ISBN: 978-0-8262-2138-4
Library of Congress Control Number: 2017953805

∞™ This paper meets the requirements of the
American National Standard for Permanence of Paper
for Printed Library Materials, Z39.48, 1984.

Typefaces: Bodoni and Jenson

Mark Twain and His Circle
Tom Quirk and John Bird, Series Editors

For Nora

Contents

Acknowledgments

I AM GRATEFUL TO Andy Barnett, the curator of the McMillan Memorial Library in Wisconsin Rapids, Wisconsin, for permission to reproduce etchings made from photographs taken by pioneer photographer H. H. Bennett in 1886; to Michelle Gray of the Warren County (Pennsylvania) Historical Society for permission to reproduce photographs from its collection; to Conor Carey, the curator at the Arabia Steamboat Museum in Kansas City, Missouri, for information about the excavation of the *Arabia*; to Joe Silva of MBI Inc. and customer services at Easton Press in Norwalk, Connecticut, for permission to reprint the Thomas Hart Benton drawing from the 1942 Limited Editions Club edition of *Huckleberry Finn*; to Rachel Aubuchon of the Saint Louis Art Museum for permission to reproduce George Caleb Bingham's 1847 painting *Raftsmen Playing Cards*; to Bill Curr, who took photographs, drew sketches, and helped arrange the various illustrations; to Calloway M'Cloud, who drew some of the sketches; to Ellen Fitzgerald of the Seattle Public Library for her engaged interest in this project and for her unstinting help in tracking down books and articles; to Marion Egge for her devoted editorial assistance with yet another project; to Judith Antonelli for her wise and careful copyediting; and to Gary Kass at the University of Missouri Press for his interest in this project and for his many helpful suggestions.

RAFTS
& Other
# RIVERCRAFT
in *Huckleberry Finn*

"On such a craft as that"

Some Basic Questions

MARK TWAIN'S *Adventures of Huckleberry Finn* has been read by more people than any other American novel. It has gone through almost one thousand editions and been translated into one hundred languages. It has been, and is still in the twenty-first century, the American novel most frequently assigned in both high school and college literature classrooms.[1] Articles and books about this novel are legion. Most criticism has focused on four controversies: allegations that Twain botched the ending of his novel, that his having Huck use the n-word so often shows that Twain and Huck were insensitive racists, that the friendship between Huck and Jim has heavy homosexual overtones, and that the raft episode should be put back in its original place in chapter 16 of *Huckleberry Finn*.

It is surprising, however, how little most readers know about the raft that carries Huck and Jim south toward Cairo, Illinois, and freedom—and then farther south from Cairo and freedom. It is surprising how little most readers know about the other kinds of rivercraft that Huck mentions.

How many of those who read, teach, and write about this amazing novel can offer more than uncertain guesses about such questions as these: What was the main purpose of Mississippi River rafts in Twain's time? What was the difference between a log raft and a lumber raft? Which kind of raft did Huck and Jim drift south on, how big was it, what kind of wood was it made of, and how much did it weigh? What was a wigwam? What did Huck and Jim's little raft actually look like? Where did Twain get the idea for Huck's lie about a smallpox victim on the raft? What was the difference between a canoe and a skiff and between a skiff and a yawl? What was the difference between a paddle and an

oar, between an oar and a steering oar, and between a steering oar and a sweep?
Why did Jim need to build an extra steering oar? What was the difference between a flatboat and a wood-flat, between a wood-flat and a woodboat, and
between a flatboat and a broadhorn? What was the difference between a scow
and a keelboat, between a keelboat and a broadhorn, and between a keelboat
and a wharfboat? What was the difference between a double-hull ferry and a
horse ferry? Was a teamboat the same as a steamboat? What fuel was used to
convert water into steam in the Mississippi steamboats in *Huckleberry Finn*?
Where and how often did the steamboats stop to refuel? What was involved in
quartering a floating vessel across the river?

Why have these basic questions so seldom been raised in the past or, if
raised, answered so sloppily? Can we claim to understand the novel if we paddle around such questions?

The premise of the first three chapters of this book is that we cannot fully
understand or appreciate Mark Twain's masterpiece if we regard such questions as peripheral, technical, unimportant, or boring. That Twain cared about
the authenticity of his novel is evident in his brief explanatory note at the start
of the novel:

> In this book a number of dialects are used, to wit: the Missouri negro dialect;
> the extremest form of the backwoods South-Western dialect; the ordinary "Pike
> County" dialect; and four modified varieties of this last. The shadings have not
> been done in a haphazard fashion, or by guess-work; but painstakingly, and with
> the trustworthy guidance and support of personal familiarity with these several
> forms of speech.
>
> I make this explanation for the reason that without it many readers would
> suppose that all these characters were trying to talk alike and not succeeding.[2]

Although it is tempting to assume that Twain is speaking tongue in cheek here,
research has shown that seven varieties of dialect can indeed be found in the
novel.[3] I propose that Twain was no less careful in his use of nautical terms. As
a boy he grew up in a Mississippi River town in Missouri called Hannibal (the
model for St. Petersburg in his novels). As a young man he worked as a Mississippi River steamboat pilot. He surely, then, knew a great deal about rafts and
rafting and about what a section of a lumber raft was. He would have known
the distinctions among an oar, a paddle, a pole, a steering oar, and a rudder.

He would have known that skiffs, canoes, keelboats, woodboats, broadhorns, wharfboats, and horse ferries were different kinds of rivercraft.

No one would think of reading Herman Melville's *Moby-Dick* without learning the basics of whaling ships, the whaling industry, and the different kinds of whales; the difference between a fast fish and a loose fish; what spermaceti was; what lays, gams, pods, try-works, and harpoon tips were; and so on. Indeed, Melville made sure that his readers learned all that as they read the novel by having his narrator Ishmael explain—often in tedious detail—all those and many more terms in the pages of the novel.

Huck is no Ishmael. He knows about Mississippi River culture because he has lived it, but he is not sophisticated enough to pause to explain his terms; he just uses them. Twain knew that it would have been out of character for Huck to do too much explaining. Huck, after all, is not a literary lad. He hates to write. He closes his book with a groan of relief: "there ain't nothing more to write about, and I am rotten glad of it, because if I'd a knowed what a trouble it was to make a book I wouldn't a tackled it, and ain't agoing to no more" (*HF* 362). Huck's failure to provide the Mississippi River equivalent of Melville's cetology chapters, however, does not mean that Twain's readers can ignore the meanings of the terms he used. The terms are important, but modern readers have to ferret the meanings out for themselves.

How can we pretend to understand *Adventures of Huckleberry Finn* if we don't even know what Huck and Jim's raft looked like, what it was made of, how it was constructed, or how deep in the water it rode? Twain might have written a second explanatory note to this effect:

In this book I assume a basic knowledge of log rafts and lumber rafts, of the different kinds of large and small rivercraft that ply the Mississippi—canoes, skiffs, wharfboats, horse ferries, trading scows, wood-flats, steamboats—and so on, as well as of the means by which they are moved: paddles, oars, steering oars, tow-ropes, and so on.

I make this explanation so that readers will not think that these rivercraft and the means to move them are all the same and that Huck Finn stupidly got them all mixed up.

Actually, Twain might have assumed a basic knowledge of the technical terms of rivercraft and river culture among his late nineteenth-century readers of

Huckleberry Finn, but more recent readers of the novel, more than a century and a half removed from its 1840s setting, need help.

Thousands of readers of the novel, of course, have for decades found much to appreciate and enjoy in *Huckleberry Finn* without knowing how Huck and Jim's raft was constructed or what a sweep was. Still, the *premise* of my first three chapters is that we cannot fully understand or deeply appreciate Twain's masterpiece if we ignore questions about rafts and other rivercraft. The *promise* of the first three chapters is to answer those questions. In doing so I have relied on three books by Mark Twain: *The Adventures of Tom Sawyer* (1876), *Life on the Mississippi* (1883), and, of course, *Adventures of Huckleberry Finn* itself (1885). I have also relied on a number of early accounts of travelers on the Mississippi River and on a number of historical accounts of the logging industry, especially in Wisconsin. In answering these questions I have found answers to still other questions, such as where Huck and Jim's raft originated and how, precisely, it would once have been joined to a much larger raft—like the large raft referred to at the start of chapter 16:

> We slept most all day, and started out, at night, a little ways behind a monstrous long raft that was as long going by as a procession. She had four long sweeps at each end, so we judged she carried as many as thirty men, likely. She had five big wigwams aboard, wide apart, and an open camp fire in the middle, and a tall flag pole at each end. There was a power of style about her. It *amounted* to something being a raftsman on such a **craft** as that. (*HF* 106)*

I pause here to explain what Twain meant by *craft*. Most dictionaries define the noun *craft* as a skill (e.g., the craft of weaving), an occupation (e.g., a carpenter's craft), or as a ship (e.g., watercraft, aircraft, or spacecraft). Of those definitions, the only one that fits the context in *Huckleberry Finn* is ship, although a raft, even a monstrously long one, is not what we think of now as a ship. The only other time Huck uses the term *craft* in the novel is in chapter 19:

> Yonder was the banks and the islands, across the water; and maybe a spark— which was a candle in a cabin window—and sometimes on the water you could

---

* All bolding of terms and phrases in quoted material for emphasis is my own.

see a spark or two—on a **raft** or a **scow**, you know; and maybe you could hear a fiddle or a song coming over from one of them **crafts**. (*HF* 158)

That sentence shows that for Twain both a raft and a scow were crafts. A couple of passages from Twain's *Life on the Mississippi* can also help us understand what Twain meant by the term *craft*:

Of course, on the great rise, down came a swarm of prodigious timber-rafts from the head waters of the Mississippi, coal barges from Pittsburg, little trading scows from everywhere, and broad-horns from "Posey County," Indiana.... Pilots bore a mortal hatred to these **craft**, and it was returned with usury. The law required all such helpless traders to keep a light burning, but it was a law that was often broken....

During this big rise these small-fry **craft** were an intolerable nuisance.[4]

For Twain a craft was almost any man-made raft or boat that floated with the current down the river. By saying that such rivercraft were "helpless," he apparently meant that for the most part they were powered only by the current, although strong men with oars could move them slightly into and out of the main channel. Twain's negative attitude here toward these crafts reflects his experiences trying to dodge them in his days as a pilot on Mississippi steamboats.

There was little consistency in the hyphenation of many of the terms used by Twain and others. We find both *flat-boat* and *flatboat*, *trading-scow* and *trading scow*, *wood-yard* and *wood yard*, *grub-stakes* and *grub stakes*, *birch-bark* and *birchbark*, and so on. Indeed, Twain himself was inconsistent in his practice. For example, he refers to both *drift-wood* (*HF* 39) and *drift wood* (*HF* 42) and to both *lumber-raft* (*HF* 44) and *lumber raft* (*HF* 60). In my quotations, of course, I have used the terms as they appear in the passages I quote, but otherwise I use what seems to be the more accepted form.

In my fourth chapter I take up the vexed question of whether modern editors of *Adventures of Huckleberry Finn* should publish what has come to be called the raft episode in chapter 16 of the novel. Twain took the episode from the unfinished manuscript of his novel and published it in chapter 3, "Frescoes from the Past," of *Life on the Mississippi*. He said that he included the episode (*LM* 240–52) "by way of illustrating keelboat talk and manners, and that now-departed and hardly-remembered raft-life" (*LM* 239). A couple of years later he included the raft episode in the newly completed manuscript of *Adventures of Huckleberry Finn* that he sent to his publisher. At his publisher's suggestion, however, Twain agreed to drop the episode from the novel so that the book would be closer in length to *The Adventures of Tom Sawyer*. Since the 1940s, editors and scholars have disagreed about whether the raft episode should be restored to its original place in chapter 16 of *Huckleberry Finn*.

In the raft episode Huck sheds his clothes and swims away from the small raft that he shares with Jim. Like a segment of a larger raft seeking to rejoin its parent raft, Huck hopes to find connection and direction among the much-admired raftsmen: "It *amounted* to something being a raftsman on such a craft as that" (*HF* 106). In the end, however, Huck is disappointed in what he actually finds on the big raft: braggarts, cowards, and a distressing story about a cruel father who murdered his infant son and buried him a barrel. Huck discovers that except perhaps for Davy, the raftsmen on such a craft as that do not amount to much of anything. Disillusioned in his search for a meaningful parent and for reliable advice about Cairo, Huck returns to his own raft and his real parent: "I swum out and got aboard, and was mighty glad to see home again" (*HF* 123).

As a child is separated from its parent, as a raft segment is separated from its parent raft, so an episode is separated from its parent novel. Huck cannot be rejoined to his biological father because that father is dead, but he can rejoin his substitute father, Jim. Huck and Jim's little raft will never be rejoined to the large raft it was once connected to because that parent raft is long gone down the river and the lumber it comprised has long been sold, but the little raft can continue to provide a home to Huck. The disconnected raft episode, separated from the novel it was written for, is the subject of chapter 4.

In my fifth chapter I reproduce in its entirety the first-person account of a "sucker" named Ceylon Childs Lincoln. *Sucker* was a slang term both for a native of Illinois (see, e.g., T. B. Thorpe's 1841 story, "The Big Bear of Arkansas") and for an inexperienced young man on his first or second journey as a raftsman. Both senses of the term apply to Lincoln. He was born in Illinois but later moved to Wisconsin, where at age eighteen, already a Civil War veteran, he signed on as a raftman, with no previous nautical experience. I close this book with a factual recollection of an older man who remembers rafting experiences about forty years earlier. It offers a nice counterpoint to the fictional recollection in *Huckleberry Finn* of another young man on his first downriver rafting journey, also around forty years earlier. It also offers a lucid description of the construction of the raft segments that were assembled in the Wisconsin headwaters, strung together end to end in rapids pieces for running the shallow and narrow upper rivers, connected side by side to make up the large Wisconsin lumber rafts, and then, farther south, connected to other Wisconsin rafts to form huge Mississippi lumber rafts like the one that Jim swims to in chapter 8 and Huck swims to in chapter 16.

Lincoln's narrative also helps us understand the psychology of the drunken, bragging, fearsome, and frightened raftsmen that Huck encounters on the huge raft in chapter 16. After learning from Lincoln about the kinds of harrowing experiences raftsmen routinely endured on the upper part of their journey, we can begin to understand why they are so afraid when they find Huck crouched among the bundles of shingles near their fire. They have just contemptuously jeered at Ed's narrative of the baby-haunted barrel. Their jeering, however, is all show. They have taken to heart Ed's story of Dick Allbright and the haunted barrel. One of the raftsmen reaches for a watermelon after Ed's narrative:

> "Boys, we'll split a watermelon on that," says the Child of Calamity; and he come rummaging around in the dark amongst the shingle bundles where I was, and put his hand on me. I was warm and soft and naked; so he says "Ouch!" and jumped back.
> "Fetch a lantern or a chunk of fire here, boys—there's a snake here as big as a cow!"
> So they run there with a lantern and crowded up and looked in on me. . . .
> "Snake him out, boys. Snatch him out by the heels." (*HF* 119–20)

They soon enough decide that Huck is not a watermelon, a cow, a snake, or a thief. They laugh again at Huck's identifying himself as the dead baby in the barrel story. Then they release him.

At the end of his long journey on the huge lumber raft, Lincoln left his fellow raftsmen and headed back home upriver. At the end of his short journey on the huge lumber raft, Huck swims back "home," where Jim is waiting for him. Provided with information he learned on the big raft, Huck soon realizes that going up the Ohio River to freedom is now impossible. He realizes that he is already at home on his crib with Jim and that his downriver journey is far from done.

CHAPTER ONE

"A little section of a lumber raft"

A Rise, a Raft, a Crib

W HAT WAS HUCK and Jim's raft like? Two recent books suggest the scope of the world's confusion about how to answer that simple question. In 2002 Lee Smith published a novel called *The Last Girls*. Most of its action takes place on a luxury tourist steamboat traveling downriver from Memphis to New Orleans in 1999. The main characters are two aging graduates of a fictional all-women's southern school named Mary Scott College. These women are a small subset of a larger group of twelve young women who, inspired by their reading of Mark Twain's *Adventures of Huckleberry Finn* about thirty-five years earlier in their sophomore Great Authors course, had decided to replicate Huck's raft journey down the Mississippi River. We learn about that earlier raft journey to New Orleans in a series of flashbacks.

In 1965 these twelve women, the "last girls" of Mary Scott College, had placed an ad in a riverboat magazine for a pilot to supervise the construction of a large raft and then to guide them on their journey south. The following fictional article from a June 10, 1965, Paducah, Kentucky, newspaper provides a succinct statement of the kind of raft the young women used for their "Huck Finn" journey south:

> PADUCAH, Ky. (AP)—"We can't believe we're finally going to do it!" were the parting words of twelve excited Mary Scott College students about to begin their "Huck Finn" journey down the Mississippi River on a raft.
>
> The adventuresome misses weighed anchor at 1:15 p.m. today, bound for New Orleans, 950 miles south. Their departure was delayed when one of the "crew" threw an anchor into the river with no rope attached, necessitating a bikini-clad

recovery operation, to the crowd's delight. "Hey, New Orleans is thataway!" shouted local wags as the ramshackle craft finally left land, hours later than planned.

Their skipper, seventy-four-year-old retired riverboat captain Gordon S. Cartwright, answered an ad that the girls had run in a riverboat magazine, writing them that he would pilot their raft down the river for nothing. He plans to make eight or nine miles an hour during daylight, tie up at night, and reach New Orleans in ten or twelve days. . . .

The raft, named the Daisy Pickett, was built by a Paducah construction company under Captain Cartwright's supervision. Resembling a floating porch, the Daisy Pickett is a forty-by-sixteen-foot wooden platform with plyboard sides, built on fifty-two oil drums and powered by two forty-horsepower motors. It cost $1800 to build. The raft has a superstructure of two-by-fours with a tarpaulin top that the "sailors" can pull up over it, mosquito netting that they can hang up, and a shower consisting of a bucket overhead with a long rope attached to it.

Living provisions are piled in corners of the raft, with army cots around the walls for sleeping. Some girls will have to sleep on the floor each night, or on land. A roughly lettered sign spelling "Galley" leads into a two-by-four plywood enclosure with canned goods, hot dog buns, and other odds and ends of food supplies. The girls will take turns on "KP duty" and have a small wood-burning stove in one corner.[1]

To call such a trip a "Huck Finn journey" is of course ludicrous on almost every level. Huck's journey was a matter of life or death, of freedom or bondage. For the "girls" of Mary Scott College, it is an expensive holiday, a game with nothing more at risk than a few mosquito bites. The *Daisy Pickett*, designed and captained by an experienced riverboat professional, is about as different from Huck's raft as possible: it is more than three times bigger and has a tarpaulin covering, a mosquito net, a galley, and a shower. It is buoyed up by a lot of empty oil barrels. Furthermore, the raft is powered by two outboard motors and so is not, as Huck and Jim's raft was, dependent on the downward pull of the river current. As we shall see, Huck and Jim's raft was nothing like the *Daisy Pickett*. Anyone who reads *The Last Girls* hoping to learn something about Huck and Jim's actual raft will be seriously misled.

When I saw a 2004 book called *Huck's Raft*, I was delighted.[2] Finally, I thought, someone was going to answer the many questions I had about the raft on which Huck and Jim make their escape from what oppresses them in

St. Petersburg: cruel parents, unfeeling slave owners, and greedy runaway-slave chasers, silly companions, and self-serving notions of what it is to be "sivilized." But no, *Huck's Raft* said almost nothing about either Huck or the raft that he and Jim share on the Mississippi. The author, Steven Mintz, never talks about the raft as a raft but only refers to it as a symbol, and then only in a few sentences like these: "The image of Huck's raft encapsulates the modern conception of childhood as a period of peril and freedom; an odyssey of psychological self-discovery and growth; and a world apart, with its own values, culture, and psychology" (5); and "Those who cannot adjust are cast adrift, to float aimlessly in a river that threatens to sink their lonely raft" (383). Furthermore, the scraggly raft in the fuzzy cover photograph (fig. 1.1) is nothing at all like the raft that Huck describes for us in his book.

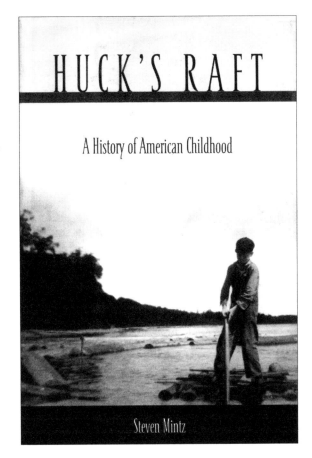

Figure 1.1. The cover of Steven Mintz's 2004 book *Huck's Raft.* This tiny and scraggly raft bears no similarity to the raft that Huck and Jim use on their Mississippi journey south.

HUCK'S RAFT

A History of American Childhood

Steven Mintz

In *Adventures of Huckleberry Finn*, the river rises and falls, the people come and go, and the scenery changes. The raft provides the only steady home that Huck and Jim know. The raft is the physical and spiritual centerpiece of the novel. Surely, then, we owe it to Mark Twain to try to answer some fundamental questions about it: What exactly was a raft? Who owned this one? Was it a log raft or a lumber raft? How was it put together? How big was it? How was it propelled? Where did it come from? How hard was it to stop such a raft once it was in motion? How much did Twain himself know about how rafts were assembled? How accurate are the many artistic renderings of Huck and Jim's raft?

Whose raft is it, anyhow?

The title *Huck's Raft* is misleading in another sense, as well, since it erases Jim's co-ownership of the raft. I prefer to call it "Huck and Jim's raft" because they found it together: "One night **we** catched a little section of a lumber raft" (*HF* 60). Later Huck refers to it as "**our** raft" (*HF* 88). After the collision with the steamboat, Jim tells Huck about how he had repaired "**our** ole raf'," to which Huck replies, "You mean to say **our** old raft warn't smashed all to flinders!" Jim explains that some of the local slaves had found the raft caught on a snag and had argued about which of them owned it the most. Jim tells Huck that he had insisted to them that the raft did not "b'long to none uv um, but to **you en me**" (*HF* 150).

Of course, legally speaking, since Huck is a minor, his share of the raft could have been claimed by his father, and Jim cannot at the start of the novel be even part owner of the raft, since it was illegal for slaves to own anything.[3] According to pre–Civil War law, then, the raft had initially belonged to Huck's pap and Miss Watson, Jim's owner. In fact, however, both Huck's pap and Miss Watson had both died early on, the former in the floating house and the latter "two months ago" (*HF* 357). Once Jim was set free in her will, he was eligible to own half the raft. During most of the time span covered in the novel, then, Huck and Jim *are* the rightful co-owners of the raft, although during most of that time neither knows it.

This is not the place to go into the technical details of maritime salvage laws, but it would appear that Huck and Jim's little raft had been abandoned by its original owner, who had no intention of trying to reclaim it. Speaking of the abandonment of "a vessel, raft, or other craft," Martin Norris wrote that "abandoning maritime property within the meaning of the salvage law is the act of leaving or deserting such property by those who were in charge of it, without hope on their part of recovering it and without the intention of returning to it."[4] Twain gave no indication that the little raft legally belonged to anyone but Huck and Jim.

What does Huck mean by the term *raft*?

We now tend to think of a raft either as a stationary floating structure held up by a flotation device of some sort and designed to provide a safe place where swimmers can rest and bask in the sun or as an inflatable boat designed to carry people down some risky rapids, as in whitewater rafting. For Huck and Jim, however, a raft was a temporary binding together of floating logs or lumber. It was designed to drift with the river current while being minimally moved or reoriented by the raftsmen. A raft was built not to carry something else but to convey itself; that is, the raft was its own cargo. A river raft was made to take advantage of the free river current to carry logs or lumber downriver to saw-mills or markets.

In Huck's time rafts usually did carry a crew, but these raftsmen were not passengers being taken to a place they wanted to visit or see. They were work-men helping to nudge a raft safely to its destination. Indeed, the men's own destination was behind them. When they had delivered the raft, the raftsmen boarded a steamboat and went back upriver to their homes, leaving the raft to be dismantled. Occasionally a piece of a raft was appropriated for other pur-poses, such as quietly helping fugitives—like boys, slaves, kings, and dukes—escape their pursuers, but that was not its original, or defining, purpose.

Huck mentions two kinds of rafts, the log raft and the lumber raft. The de-fining purpose of a log raft was to float logs to a sawmill to be turned into lum-ber. A log raft was typically a single log in thickness, so could be floated down very shallow rivers. The defining purpose of a lumber raft was to float milled planks, boards, and beams to a town downriver to be dismantled and turned into houses, barns, bridges, boats, or furniture. A lumber raft was usually about two feet thick and so could be launched only on rivers that were deep or that became deep when rain or upstream melting snow made them so.

Early in *Huckleberry Finn*, while he is living with his pap in an old log shanty on the Illinois side of the Mississippi River three miles upstream from St. Pe-tersburg, Huck notices that the river has begun to rise:

> I noticed some pieces of limbs and such things floating down, and a sprinkling of bark; so I knowed the river had begun to rise. I reckoned I would have great

times, now, if I was over at the town. The June rise used to be always luck for me; because as soon as that rise begins, here comes cord-wood floating down, and **pieces of log rafts**—sometimes a dozen logs together; so all you have to do is to catch them and sell them to the wood yards and the sawmill. (*HF* 37)

What was a log raft?

A log raft was made up of floating round lengths of tree trunk with the bark still intact but with the limbs cut off. The logs were fastened or corralled together, not to carry people or cargo but because the logs themselves had to be held together as they drifted downstream to a sawmill. Twain wrote in *Life on the Mississippi* of the danger that log rafts posed for steamboats:

> Sometimes, in the big river, when we would be feeling our way cautiously along through a fog, the deep hush would suddenly be broken by yells and a clamor of tin pans, and all in an instant a **log raft** would appear vaguely through the webby veil, close upon us; and then we did not wait to swap knives, but snatched our engine-bells out by the roots and piled on all the steam we had, to scramble out of the way! One doesn't hit a rock or a **solid log raft** with a steamboat when he can get excused. (*LM* 292)

Occasionally a small log raft was used for other purposes before it could be joined to other small rafts to make one big raft or before it was dismantled at a sawmill. For example, in chapter 13 of *The Adventures of Tom Sawyer*, Tom, Huck, and Joe Harper become "pirates" by "capturing" just above St. Petersburg "a small log raft."[5] Because it is not said to be a piece, a part, a fragment, a section, or a segment of a larger raft, and because it already has steering oars in place fore and aft, we can safely assume that it had been built as a separate raft and guided down a narrow or shallow tributary to the big river.

Charles Russell, one of the early historians of the rafting industry, wrote about a raftsman named Stephen Hanks who in the winter of 1837–1838 went out to cut trees along the upper Mississippi River to supply the sawmill of a relative. He cut the trees into sawlogs and then made them "into rafts, little rafts, eight or ten logs in each, and helped to float them down to the mill."[6] The small log raft that Tom Sawyer's "pirates" "capture" was apparently a raft like that. Tom and his fellow pretend pirates use the steering oars to maneuver their raft out to the middle of the Mississippi and then to land it on Jackson's Island. They leave it there and go ashore. Soon a rise in the river carries it off. It is found some days later washed up on the riverbank five or six miles below St. Petersburg. What the boys used as a pretend pirate ship had apparently been built merely to be floated to a sawmill.

The logs in the log rafts that Huck describes in *Huckleberry Finn* are sawlogs—that is, round logs with the branches cut off, most commonly in lengths of twelve or sixteen feet, ready to be made into lumber in a sawmill. These logs were typically held together in rafts by long poles attached crosswise and by ropes, chains, or (later) steel cables. Large log rafts could be very large indeed (fig. 1.2), far too large and heavy for a boy in a canoe or a skiff to tow. Besides, a large log raft would have been manned by raftsmen who would have prevented Huck from taking it.

Figure 1.2. A large log raft. The sawlogs were corralled to keep them together as they floated downriver. Note particularly the long steering oar, or sweep, at the near (stern or aft) end of the raft. Less visible at the far (front or fore) end is another just like it. The current would have propelled the raft downstream. The sweeps were designed merely to move the raft sideways so as to keep it in the main channel, to move it to the shore for mooring, or to steer the raft away from collisions. Note also the rope that tethers the raft to the riverbank until the raftsmen are ready to cast off and start the day's journey downriver. A log raft drew (i.e., extended below the surface) only a few inches of water, so it could move in shallow rivers like this one. Lumber rafts drew almost two feet of water. These logs were probably on their way to a sawmill downriver, where they would be sawed up and made into lumber rafts with a far deeper draw. This photo was most likely taken around 1905 on the west branch of the Susquehanna River near Westport in Clinton County, Pennsylvania.

It is important to notice that Huck speaks of finding "**pieces** of log rafts." Sometimes a large log raft would hit a snag, a rock, or an island, or be struck by a steamboat, and have a piece torn away. Walter A. Blair describes such a collision: "One of the Northern Line packets, going up river in the night, ran into a raft, under way, and did it considerable damage. George Tromley, the pilot of the raft, made a claim on the Packet Company, when he delivered his raft to Saint Louis. . . . The bill was then promptly paid, with costs."[7] The owner of a damaged large log raft would have had good financial reason to keep his men on the larger raft, abandoning the smaller pieces of just a few logs. Abandoned pieces of log rafts were in theory the property of the company that cut them, fastened them together, and floated them downriver, but in practice they were often abandoned and so considered salvage by those who could "catch" them and tow them to a local sawmill. The owners of the sawmills were not fussy about asking for proof of ownership. They were happy to pay cash for good sawlogs.

One afternoon Huck and his pap go out to the riverbank to see what the rising Mississippi has brought them:

> The river was coming up pretty fast, and lots of drift-wood going by on the rise. By and by, along comes **part of a log raft**—nine logs fast together. We went out with the skiff and towed it ashore. Then we had dinner. Anybody but pap would a waited and seen the day through, so as to catch more stuff; but that warn't pap's style. Nine logs was enough for one time; he must shove right over to town and sell. (*HF* 39)

A river on the rise picked up lots of useless wood—limbs, branches, and stumps—that Jim and Huck refer to as "drift-wood" (*HF* 39, 42, 54), but floating sawlogs and log rafts were not useless. They represented cash in hand.

In Huck's time sawmills were often situated on riverbanks. There were three reasons for this. First, the early upper-river sawmills ran on water power, using either a waterwheel or a water turbine. Steam-powered sawmills replaced water-powered ones, especially on the lower Mississippi, where the river was wide, the current was slower, and the water level fluctuated greatly. Tom Sawyer's uncle, Silas Phelps, is said to own and run "a little steam sawmill that was on the bank" (*HF* 271). Second, the river brought to the sawmill floating sawlogs and log rafts from upriver. Third, the river gave the sawmill operators a way to float the sawed lumber downriver to markets. The Mississippi and its upper tributaries, then, provided not only cheap energy to run the sawmills but also cheap transportation for log rafts coming in from upriver and for lumber rafts going downriver to markets like St. Louis and New Orleans. The key feature of the Mississippi River was that it *moved*. What floated on it moved also.

As soon as his pap disappears across the river to sell his nine-log raft to the sawmill, Huck makes his escape in the drift canoe he had previously retrieved from the Mississippi. Early the next morning he finds himself at the head of Jackson's Island. It is still dark, but from his vantage point he can see a big raft in the moonlight:

> A **monstrous big lumber-raft** was about a mile up stream, coming along down, with a lantern in the middle of it. I watched it come creeping down, and when it was most abreast of where I stood, I heard a man say, "Stern oars, there!—heave her head to stabboard [starboard, or right]!" (*HF* 44)

What was a lumber raft?

Sawlogs were the wood that went into a sawmill. Lumber was the wood that came out of a sawmill: beams, posts, planks, and boards. A lumber raft was not a boat or a barge made to *haul* lumber; rather, it was a floating structure or craft *built* of lumber. When the lumber raft reached its destination, it was not unloaded; it was dismantled. Some of the lumber rafts did carry lumber products, like bundles of shingles—thin tapered slices used for layered roofing and siding—and laths, narrow strips used as base for plastering. When Huck visits the big lumber raft in chapter 16, he crawls "amongst some bundles of shingles on the weather side of the fire" (*HF* 107). According to Robert Fries, "Pioneer lumber camps usually converted part of their logs into . . . shingles . . . made by hand in a building constructed for the purpose. Taking a pine log of particularly straight grain, the shingle maker sawed it into blocks, which he then split into thin pieces with an instrument called a 'frow.'"[8]

The big "raff" on which Jim makes his escape from St. Petersburg in chapter 8 was also a lumber raft, to judge by its large size and its plank surface. This is how Jim describes his encounter with the raft:

> "I see a light a-comin' roun' de p'int bymeby, so I wade' in en shove' a log ahead o' me en swum more'n half way acrost de river en got in 'mongst de drift wood, en

kep' my head down low en kinder swum agin de current tell de raff come along. Den I swum to de stern uv it en tuck a'holt. It clouded up en 'uz pooty dark for a little while. So I clumb up en laid down on de **planks**. De men 'uz **all 'way yonder** in de middle, whah de lantern wuz." (*HF* 53–54)

Some log rafts on the Mississippi could be very large, but while a large log raft might have a small area near the center covered with planks for the comfort of the raftsmen, the planks would never have extended "all 'way" to the edge, where Jim was. This one, then, must have been a lumber raft, not a log raft.

Raftsmen on large rafts often tied up at the riverbank at night to avoid collisions, but when they did move at night they were always supposed to suspend a lantern from a post near the center of the raft so that steamboats coming up or down the river could avoid them. Upriver steamboats were less of a threat than downriver ones. The rafts would naturally stay right in the middle of the main channel because that is where the current was swiftest. These rafts were rarely threatened by upstream steamboats, which avoided the swift current and headed for the "easy" water at the sides of the river. But downstream steamboats wanted to stay right in the middle of the channel, where the rafts were, so they could take advantage of the current to speed them along. The lights at the center of both the raft that Huck saw and the one that Jim swam to were lanterns designed primarily not to illuminate the raft for the benefit of the raftsmen but to announce their location to downstream steamboats, which would then— they hoped—steer around them.

How were "cribs" and lumber rafts constructed?

The lumber rafts that Huck and Jim see drifting at night past St. Petersburg are very large. Lumber rafts were not, however, so large at their upstream point of origin. A large lumber raft would have been made up of many small sections, or cribs, each of which, in the 1840s, was typically twelve feet wide and sixteen feet long. (Later the cribs were generally sixteen feet square.) Each crib was built separately and launched separately.

Crib assemblers started each crib with nine strong saplings—preferably either hickory or oak—two inches in diameter. From these saplings they shaped pins roughly the size of baseball bats, called grub stakes, grub pins, or just grubs. They were called that because they were grubbed, or dug out of the ground with the roots attached. Most of the roots were eventually cut off, but enough had to be left on so that the grub stake was larger at the bottom than at the top. The grub stakes were cut to be about three or four feet long (fig. 1.3).

When they had the nine grub stakes ready, the crib assemblers selected three two-inch-thick foundation planks. Sometimes called grub planks, these foundation planks were usually at least eight inches wide and sixteen feet long. The assemblers also selected three eight-inch planks twelve feet long. Four inches in from each end of all six of these foundation planks, the crib assemblers drilled a hole two inches in diameter, and they drilled another two-inch hole in the center of each plank. In the sixteen-foot grub planks they tapered the nine holes to receive the tapered bottoms of the grub stakes. The purpose of the tapering was both to keep the grub stakes from pulling up through the hole and to prevent them from protruding so far below the foundation plank that they would catch on stones, snags, or sandbars. The front ends of the sixteen-foot grub planks

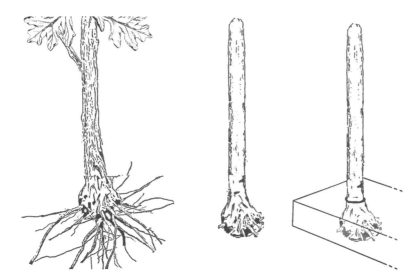

Figure 1.3. Grub stakes. These were usually made of hickory or oak saplings that were grubbed, or dug out of the ground with the roots attached. They were two inches in diameter and three to four feet long. The drawing shows, from left to right, the grub stake as it was grubbed, the grub stake with the roots and the bark shaved off, and the grub stake in a foundation plank. The hole in the foundation plank would have been tapered—that is, made wider at the bottom than at the top. The primary purpose of the funnel-shaped hole was to provide a secure seat for the tapered grub stake. The secondary purpose of the tapered hole in the bottom was to prevent the grub stake from sticking so far below the foundation plank that it might catch on a rock, a submerged log, or a sandbar.

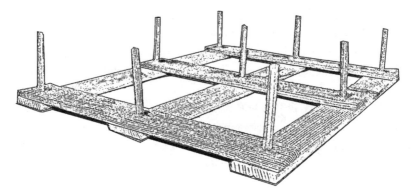

Figure 1.4. Foundation planks. The planks for a lumber raft were predrilled with two-inch holes to receive the grub stakes. They held the nine stakes in place as the crib assemblers stacked the crib until it was about two feet thick. The three bottom, or foundation, grub planks were sixteen feet long. The next layer, set crosswise to the ones below, were planks twelve feet long. The thickness of the planks could vary as long as the planks in each layer were the same thickness.

were beveled (cut at an angle) so that they would tend to bounce up or glance off if the crib hit a rock or other underwater impediment.

The next step was to lay out the basic crib frame. The assemblers would put grub stakes in the holes in each of the sixteen-foot grub planks and turn them so that the flared or beveled ends of the grub stakes were down while the grub stakes stuck vertically up through the planks. The assemblers then placed the three twelve-foot planks crosswise down over the upright grub stakes. That gave them the basic rectangular shape of the crib (fig. 1.4).

The assemblers then stacked the crib with one- or two-inch-thick planks, each layer laid crosswise to the one below it and the one above it. The planks that coincided with the grub stakes were also drilled to fit down over the grub stakes, although occasionally the drilling could be skipped if a plank ended just at a grub stake. In that case the plank could be notched with an axe or a hatchet to fit around the grub stake. The thickness of the planks could vary as long as all the planks in each layer were the same thickness. When the stack was two feet thick, the crib builders took three one-by-eights or two-by-eights (sometimes four- or even eight-by-eights), known as binder planks or witch planks, and drilled two-inch holes in them to match the ones below in the foundation grub planks. The binder planks were placed over the grub stakes parallel to the foundation planks at the bottom of the crib (fig. 1.5).

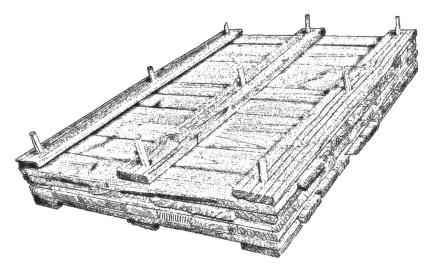

Figure 1.5. The completed crib. The top layer consisted of three binder planks, also predrilled with two-inch holes. These planks were "witched" (i.e., squeezed and wedged) down to keep the crib tight together on its downstream journey. Notice that the grub stakes all extend above the surface. They were used to join one crib to other cribs just like it. The middle one on the front and the back could serve as a pivot for a steering oar.

In 1886 the Arpin family of Grand Rapids (later named Wisconsin Rapids) sent a fleet of rafts down the river during the spring high water. Near Wisconsin Dells the family members were joined by pioneer photographer H. H. Bennett, who documented their life in photographs as they passed through the Dells and on down to the Mississippi River. A book entitled *Story of a Raftsman's Life on the Wisconsin River* is a collection of almost forty etchings made from Bennett's photographs.[9] The etchings, which are accessible on the McMillan Memorial Library's Flickr site, are remarkably faithful to the photographs. I am grateful to the McMillan Memorial Library for permission to reprint a number of the etchings in this and the next chapter.

As the etchings show, the crib builders would use a lever to "witch" the crib: The lever was clamped or chained onto one of the protruding grub stakes and leveraged down to squeeze the lumber tight against the foundation grub plank. When it was tight, the assemblers made a small vertical gash in the grub stake just above the surface of the binder plank and hammered into the gash a "witch"—a narrow wooden wedge. That wedge would split the grub stake, thus widening it enough to keep the tension tight. Then the assemblers moved on to the next grub stake. When they had witched each of the nine grub stakes, the crib was pinched tight enough that the boards would not slip out, especially after the crib was launched and the lumber swelled up from being in the water (figs. 1.6 and 1.7).

Figure 1.6. Witching the binder plank. The raftsmen here are performing one of the last steps in constructing a lumber crib. An iron loop is placed over the exposed grub stake. It is attached to an eight-foot-long lever. The lever is positioned over a vertical notched fulcrum board. At the other end of the lever sits a raftsman. His weight simultaneously pulls the grub stake up and pushes the binder plank down. When there is no more give, the kneeling raftsman drives a wedge into the exposed part of the grub stake, thus holding the two-foot-thick stack of lumber tight. This etching and several of those below were made from photographs taken by H. H. Bennett in 1886. (Courtesy of the McMillan Memorial Library, Wisconsin Rapids)

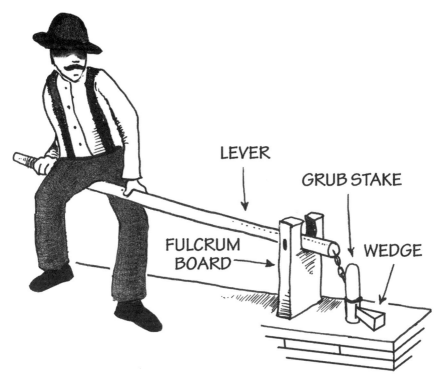

Figure 1.7. Detail of witch. This drawing shows more clearly how the witch worked to compress the layers of the crib. As weight was applied to the end of the lever, the grub stake was pulled up as the binder plank was simultaneously pushed down. To hold the crib tight, a vertical gash was cut into the lower part of the exposed grub stake and a hardwood wedge was driven in horizontally. It tended to split the grub stake slightly to keep the tension on the binder plank. Alternatively, the wedge might be driven in vertically alongside the grub stake, thus applying pressure between the grub stake and the side of the two-inch hole.

Sometimes the cribs were built in special sheds, sometimes on sloping riverbanks, sometimes on tilting cradles, and sometimes, in the winter, right on the river ice to await the spring thaw. When the raft pilot decided that the river was right for rafting, the completed cribs were shifted end to end into strings of six or seven cribs. Each crib was joined to the next one in the string by means of two additional planks with holes drilled into them at proper distances so that at least one hole fit over a grub stake on one of the cribs and at least two fit over two grub stakes on the next one (fig. 1.8). The six or seven cribs so joined end to end in a string were known as rapids pieces. A rapids piece was narrow enough to be handled by two oarsmen, one at the front of the first crib and one at the rear of the last crib. The string was flexible enough that it could usually survive the undulations of a fast ride down a slide, or rapids (fig. 1.9). A slide was an overflow channel designed to permit rafts to go around a dam.

Figure 1.8. Two cribs joined end to end. This drawing shows the way two cribs were joined together merely by dropping two predrilled planks down over the grub stakes that were left sticking up for just that purpose. When six or seven cribs were so joined together into a string, the result was called a rapids piece—so named because it was slender enough to be able to run a narrow rapids in a small river.

Once the rapids pieces had passed successfully through the shallow upper reaches of the tributaries of the Mississippi and had made it down to the safer—that is, wider and deeper—part of the river, they could be joined side by side with other rapids pieces to form a larger raft, often called a Wisconsin raft or, further downriver, a Mississippi raft. The rapids pieces or strings were coupled to other strings by means of short yokes drilled with two or three carefully spaced two-inch-wide holes. Often made of round-topped slabs from the sawmill, these yokes fit down over the protruding grub stakes of adjacent cribs to hold them tight together (figs. 1.10 and 1.11).[10]

Figure 1.9. Running a slide on a rapids piece. The raftsman on the front of this string of cribs had the dangerous responsibility of using the front sweep, or steering oar, to guide the raft away from shoals, rocks, and other obstructions. In this etching the raftsman pushes down on the dry end of the steering oat to keep the wet end from smashing into a rock. A slide was a low spot in a river dam designed to allow passage for rapids pieces if the water level was high enough. (Courtesy of the McMillan Memorial Library, Wisconsin Rapids)

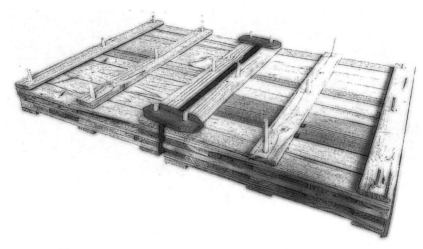

Figure 1.10. Two cribs yoked side by side. This drawing shows the way two identical cribs could be yoked side by side with short yokes predrilled to fit over adjacent grub stakes.

Mark Twain said in *Life on the Mississippi* that the larger lumber rafts were "an acre or so" (*LM* 239). It would take approximately 225 of the cribs I have described to make up such a raft. A sixteen-by-twelve-foot crib had a top surface of 192 square feet. Thus 225 of those cribs would cover 43,200 square feet, or almost an acre (43,560 square feet). Fries reported that after the Civil War, three- and four-acre rafts were not uncommon.[11] The larger rafts probably had slightly larger cribs—the norm in later years was a crib sixteen feet on a side— but the greater number of cribs joined together, not the size of the individual cribs, accounted for most of the increased acreage (fig. 1.12).

There was some variation in the way cribs were built. Depending on the size of the lumber available at a particular sawmill at a particular time and the needs of downriver clients, a sawmill might build a set of narrower cribs (e.g., eight or ten feet wide) as long as they made a sufficient number of a given width that they could connect end to end to make a series of rapids pieces. Some sawmills sometimes made cribs with only two foundation planks and two binder planks, eliminating the set that usually ran down the center of the crib. George Caleb Bingham's 1847 painting *Raftsmen Playing Cards* (discussed in chapter 2) shows such a crib. As we shall see in chapter 5, Ceylon Childs Lincoln's cribs were made with only two sets of foundation and binder planks. Eliminating the center set of foundation binder planks would have weakened the crib and made

Figure 1.11. Joining two strings. This etching shows two strings, or rapids pieces, each having just run the slide shown in figure 1.9, being maneuvered together so they could run the next section of river as a larger raft. If they encountered other narrows or shallows ahead, the strings could be unyoked and run by or through the obstruction separately. (Courtesy of the McMillan Memorial Library, Wisconsin Rapids)

Figure 1.12. A two-string lumber raft. The left and right strings were joined by short yoking boards slipped down over the protruding grub stakes. The cribs were joined front to back by longer boards that slipped lengthwise over the grub stakes. The steering oars were so long and heavy that it took two men to move the one in the left foreground. The dapper gentleman in the bowler hat is presumably the raft pilot. The photo was taken in the late 1800s on the Allegheny River. (Courtesy of the Warren County Historical Society, Pennsylvania)

it more vulnerable to damage. Perhaps to compensate for the elimination of the center foundation binder set, his sawmill used heavier planks—two-by-twelve-inch planks, not the skimpier two-by-eight-inch ones that I described above. In addition, lathe-turned grub stakes eventually replaced hand-dug grub stakes, and different sawmills had their own variations on how to do the witching.

How were the cribs separated at the end of the journey?

The design of the crib as the basic unit of the lumber raft was brilliant. Cribs could be made in uniform dimensions of twelve-by-sixteen or sixteen-by-sixteen feet. These cribs could then be quickly joined to other cribs just by slipping predrilled boards or short yokes over the protruding grub stakes that stuck up above the surface of the binder planks. Cribs thus joined could then be separated easily by lifting the joining planks or yokes for long enough to get through a rapids or off a sandbar, then rejoined to other cribs and strings. And when a large lumber raft got to a destination, the cribs could be separated for sale to customers (fig. 1.13). Some customers might want only one crib, and some might want a dozen. Blair described his father's buying cribs: "My father was engaged in a retail lumber business, first in Galena, and afterwards in Princeton, a smaller town, on the Mississippi. He secured all his supply from floating rafts that would land above our yard so we could pick out the cribs and strings that had the kinds of lumber we wanted for our trade."[12]

To get access to the lumber, the new owners of the crib had only to cut or otherwise remove the witch wedges, hit the exposed grub stakes with a heavy sledgehammer to drive them out through the bottom of the foundation grub plank, and then just peel off the layers of boards. Or they might just saw off the tops of the grub stakes and lift the boards up. Some of the planks did have two-inch holes in them, but those holes did not affect the structural integrity

Figure 1.13. Dismantling lumber cribs. This photograph shows two raftsmen taking apart a couple of lumber cribs on the banks of the Allegheny River in Pennsylvania in the late 1800s. As they took the planks up, they loaded them onto the nearby wagon. (Courtesy of the Warren County Historical Society, Pennsylvania)

of the plank. Indeed, a twentieth-century resident of Hannibal, Missouri, said that those holes were something to brag about:

> Rafted lumber gave the town [of Hannibal] its start, and literally built it into a trading center in the 1840s. . . . If you have an old house, you may find two-inch holes in the joists, rafters, or frame. Our basement ceiling, which used to be the joists of the house before we added the basement, is full of such holes. These holes are excellent for storing ball bats, threading extension cords, or hiding matches and keys from the children. That lumber is par excellent Wisconsin pine, cut from virgin stands of timber which will never again be found in America.[13]

In chapter 16 of *Huckleberry Finn*, Huck leaves Jim on their little raft and paddles his canoe out to try to discover how far they are from Cairo. Before he gets very far he encounters two slave traders. One of them asks Huck, "What's that, yonder?" Huck replies, "**A piece of a raft**" (*HF* 125). Later, in chapter 20, when the king and the duke come aboard, Huck has to invent a lie about how he and Jim happened to be alone on the raft. He says that he, his pap, his little brother Ike, and their slave Jim needed to get from Missouri to a little town below New Orleans. They did not have enough money, Huck says, to take a steamboat: "Well, when the river rose pa had a streak of luck, one day; he ketched **this piece of a raft**; so we reckoned we'd go down to Orleans on it" (*HF* 166). There is no doubt, then, that Huck knows that his raft is not a full raft but just a piece of one.

Is Huck and Jim's raft a piece of a log raft or of a lumber raft?

Huck had earlier given an unequivocal answer to the question of whether the piece of raft was from a log raft or a lumber raft. After some days on Jackson's Island, he and Jim manage to secure the piece of a raft that is to be their home for the next several weeks:

> One night we catched **a little section of a lumber raft**—nice pine planks. It was twelve foot wide and about fifteen or sixteen foot long, and the top stood above water six or seven inches, a solid, level floor. (*HF* 60)

Huck says in plain English that the raft they had caught was part of a lumber raft. He uses the word *section* rather than *crib*, but the dimensions—twelve feet by sixteen feet—leave no doubt what he is talking about.

In his introduction to the raft episode, which Twain had lifted from the un-finished manuscript of *Huckleberry Finn* and printed in *Life on the Mississippi*, he used the word *fragment* rather than *piece, section*, or *crib*, but he again iden-tified it as part of a lumber raft: "They have found **a fragment of a lumber raft** (it is high water and dead summer-time)" (*LM* 239). As a former Mississippi River pilot, Twain would certainly have known about the Wisconsin origins of many of the lumber rafts he had had to dodge. In *Life on the Mississippi* he reported that some former keelboatmen sometimes took a job "on a pine-raft constructed in the forests up toward the sources of the Mississippi" (*LM* 239). He later mentioned that when the Mississippi was "on the great rise, down came a swarm of prodigious timber-rafts from the headwaters of the Missis-sippi" (*LM* 290). Twain apparently used the term *timber raft* synonymously with *lumber raft*.

He would surely have known that sections of these large Wisconsin and Mis-sissippi rafts were sometimes separated—either on purpose or by accident—from the larger raft. He would have known at least some of what another Mississippi pilot, W. H. Glover, later wrote about the dangers that might cause a crib to be separated from its parent raft:

The test of this formidably constructed raft came immediately upon starting its journey to the Mississippi market towns. The rapids, dams, and eddies of the upper Wisconsin could tear apart rafts that almost nothing else could shake. . . .

The rafts were run during the flood seasons. A heavy flow of water was needed to carry rafts over both the rapids of the upper Wisconsin and the shifting sand bars of the lower river. . . .

Dams were a serious danger. They were provided with slides usually about fifty feet wide to help the raft pass. . . .

The hazards of passing over these slides are plainly realized in retrospect. The least of them was the possibility of sticking on the slide when the flow was too slight to give the piece a good start. But when two feet of water was roaring over the dam, the slightest miscalculation could fatally misdirect the piece in spite of frantic efforts of the oarsmen to head it straight between the piers. . . . They sad-dlebagged the pier at the opening of the slide but jumped to it and were rescued by boat—a daring feat which was routine to raftsmen. The fate of the raft was, of course, pretty complete destruction. Many were smashed in this way, some were actually carried over the dam itself, and in a few instances they were com-pletely somersaulted. Striking the gunwale at the side of the slide was extremely dangerous also. A good deal of the lumber was recovered, although the lower Wisconsin was strewn with the remains of rafts. . . .

Even normal passage over slides had its thrills. Many watched, but few wanted to ride the rafts. . . .

The [rapids] pieces plunged under water on leaving the slide. When the raft nosed into the slide, the oars were swung up and made fast with rope halters and the crew threw themselves flat and grabbed for the "sucker line"—a rope strung down the center of the piece. Instances were reported of rafts missing the slide but plunging safely over the dam—further proof of the strength of the rapids piece.[14]

Twain never said precisely what caused Huck and Jim's "little section of a lumber raft" to separate from its parent raft, but any reader who knew how lumber rafts were constructed and about the perils they faced on their downstream journey could have imagined several destructive scenarios. In fact, however, because so few readers of *Huckleberry Finn* have known anything about lumber rafts, the cribs from which they were built up, or how susceptible they were to serious damage in the rapids, dams, storms, and eddies of the upper rivers, virtually all readers have mistakenly read Huck and Jim's little section of a lumber raft as a piece of a log raft with a top skin of pine planks. One exception was Charles Russell, who said in a footnote to his description of the building of cribs, "A little by-way incident in American literature pertains to this operation. In *Huckleberry Finn*, Huck and Jim Watson, the Negro, capture a crib from a lumber raft that has come to grief near Hannibal, Missouri. Jim takes up some of the boards and makes a wigwam, and on the crib as a raft they live and float down the river."[15] Russell means, of course, St. Petersburg, the name of Huck's hometown in the novel, but Twain does not say that the parent lumber raft had "come to grief."

Typical of the confusion about the rafts in *Huckleberry Finn* is Michael Hearn's definition of the nine-log "part of a log raft" (*HF* 39) that pap sells to the sawmill in St. Petersburg as a "crib."[16] A crib was associated with a lumber raft, not a log raft. Also typical is Kent Rasmussen's statement that Huck and Jim's raft has "a pine-plank deck."[17] That way of putting it implies that the pine planks are to be found only as a top layer and that what is under that "deck" is not more pine planks. Twain, of course, says nothing about a deck. The confusion of a log raft and a lumber raft is also evident in the SparkNotes online "translation" of *Huckleberry Finn*. Twain's "One night we caught a little section of a lumber raft—nice pine planks" is "translated" as "One night we caught a small portion of a log raft made out of some fine pine planks."[18] A log raft was made of logs, not planks. A lumber raft was made of planks, not logs. Huck and Jim's crib has no logs in it, on it, or under it.

How much does Huck and Jim's crib weigh?

Huck gives precise dimensions for his and Jim's crib: the surface is twelve feet by fifteen or sixteen feet—a standard crib size. In a 1944 report to the Public Service Commission of Wisconsin, Adolph Kenneberg wrote that a "Wisconsin lumber raft was composed of what were called cribs. Six cribs yoked together constituted a rapids-piece. Three rapids-pieces placed side by side made up a Wisconsin raft. The cribs were either sixteen by twelve feet or sixteen feet square."[19]

Huck says that Huck and Jim's raft is made of pine planks and that six or seven inches show above the waterline. Assuming that around three-quarters of the raft—eighteen inches—is below the waterline, the raft would be about two feet thick. In an engaging essay, Michael Powell describes the sort of raft that Twain would have seen as a boy in Hannibal:

> Early in July 1844, author-to-be Mark Twain, then eight years old, was in place to see the introduction of commercial lumber rafting as it passed his Missouri home on the west bank of the Mississippi River: first, rafts of two-feet-thick old-growth Wisconsin, Minnesota, and Michigan white pine (*Pinus strobus*), sawn into mill-standard sixteen-foot lengths, gathered from the Mississippi's upper tributaries; then, as mills sprang up along the way, rafts of . . . milled lumber, cross-planked "cribs" corner-pinned together, drawing a foot-and-a-half to two feet of water.[20]

A raft of newly sawed lumber packed tight into a block 16 feet long, 12 feet wide, and 2 feet thick would total 384 cubic feet. The US Forest Service has published charts showing the weight per cubic foot of more than 150 American woods, both green and air-dried. The lumber raft in *Huckleberry Finn* would, of course, be made up of green (i.e., freshly sawed) planks. Green *Pinus strobus*, one of the lightest woods, weighed 36 pounds per cubic foot. Huck and Jim's crib, then, would weigh about 13,824 pounds, or almost seven tons.[21]

In addition to the weight of the lumber, there is the weight of Huck and Jim's equipment, the six inches of dirt under the fire, and the men traveling on the raft, all of which easily pushes the total weight to more than seven tons.

How easy was it to stop a raft?

Seven tons is a lot of weight. That Huck and Jim's raft was so heavy helps us to understand why it "broke loose" from its tie-up on the wreck of the *Walter Scott* in chapter 12. Jim tells Huck, "Raf'? Dey ain' no raf' no mo', she done **broke loose** en gone!" (*HF* 85). Its weight also helps us to understand why in chapter 15 Huck cannot stop the raft from getting away from him:

> Well, the second night a fog begun to come on, and we made for a tow-head to tie to, for it wouldn't do to try to run in fog; but when I paddled ahead in the canoe, with the line, to make fast, there warn't anything but little saplings to tie to. I passed the line around one of them right on the edge of the cut bank, but there was a stiff current and the raft come booming down so lively she **tore it out by the roots** and away she went. (*HF* 99)

It would have been hard indeed to stop a seven-ton raft that was being carried along by a swift current (fig. 1.14). It was generally known that raftsmen often had trouble stopping—sometimes called snubbing or checking—their rafts.

Several early travelers and commentators discussed the problem of stopping rafts on the Mississippi:

> The next thing that afforded us amusement was a long raft of boards and shingles, which was intended for this place [Natchez]. The owners expected its arrival, and were on the Levee to see it landed in safety, but it was soon discovered that it would not be able to reach even the eddy. They accordingly mustered all the ropes and boats which could be readily collected, and while those on the raft sent their boats and ropes ashore, these went off with theirs; but the power of the raft was so great, and the current so strong, that the ropes all snapped like threads; nor were they able to make a landing before they had drifted five miles below the city.[22]

No one had yet devised a satisfactory way to moor a raft, or, in river language, "check" it. They tied one end of a rope to the raft and took the whole line ashore, wrapping the other end several times around a tree. When the line went taut it frequently pulled the tree out by its roots. Sometimes the line broke and then the end, flying through the air, became a perilous missile.[23]

The ponderous raft was not easy to stop once it had headway. Trees used for snubbing posts were sometimes torn up by the roots.[24]

How much did Twain himself know about how rafts were assembled?

In an early draft of *Huckleberry Finn*, Huck and Jim's raft was utterly destroyed when it was struck by the steamboat at the end of what became chapter 16: "she come smashing through the raft and tore it to toothpicks and splinters" (HF 425).[25] In the final version, however, Twain decided that he had more work for the raft to do, so he revised that to read simply, "she come smashing straight through the raft" (*HF* 130). Later Huck learns from Jim that some local slaves had found the raft hung up on a snag and had brought it in to shore. Jim tells Huck that one end of the raft was "tore up a good deal—one en' of

Figure 1.14. Checking a lumber raft. This etching shows three men about to stop ("check" or "snub") a floating raft for the night. The raftsman on the left is about to toss the line to the man on the shore, who would tie it around a tree. The barefoot raftsman would then snub the other end around one of the grub stakes and hope the raft would come to a stop. Sometimes it did. (Courtesy of the McMillan Memorial Library, Wisconsin Rapids)

her was—but dey warn't no great harm done" and that he had her "all fixed up agin mos' as good as new" (*HF* 150). Twain left unanswered certain questions about what damage the collision had done to the raft when the steamboat had smashed right through it: whether the grub stakes had been pulled loose, the fore steering oar destroyed, or the wigwam damaged; where had Jim gotten the tools and the lumber he would have needed to repair the raft; and so on.

To return to one of the questions I started with: Why have such basic questions about Huck and Jim's raft so seldom been asked in the past or, if asked, answered so sloppily? Three obvious answers present themselves. The first is that readers have not bothered to follow Twain's clues about the nature of Huck and Jim's raft and have not done even the most basic research about what a little section of a lumber raft might have looked like, how it was put together, and in what sense it might once have been part of a much larger raft.

The second answer is that Huck, an "ignorant village boy" (*LM* 239), either does not know or is not much interested in explaining such details. He wants to ride the raft to freedom, not analyze how it was put together or speculate on how it became separated from whatever large raft it might once have been part of up in Wisconsin.

The third possibility is that Twain himself was perhaps somewhat uncertain about what this little section of a lumber raft was, where it came from, how it was constructed, or how Jim would have repaired it after the collision with a steamboat. Twain knew rafts from looking down on them from the pilot house of a steamboat that was trying to dodge them. He apparently had little personal knowledge of the upriver sawmills that sawed the lumber that went into the rafts, the way they were built, or the way small rafts were yoked to make huge rafts. Surely, then, Twain himself must bear some responsibility for the confusion that readers and illustrators have demonstrated. Had he understood better than he did how a lumber crib was put together, he would not have had Jim build a wigwam with planks taken up from the top layer of boards. He would have described the grub stakes and their important function in holding the crib together and in providing a pivot for the fore and aft steering oars. He would have written more specifically about how one end of the raft was "tore up" by the steamboat and what Jim had to do to repair it.

Bernard DeVoto said the following about *Adventures of Huckleberry Finn*:

The novel's greatness need not be argued. The framework is faulty, the joinery is unskillful, the movement is sometimes aimless, and from time to time Mark's lack of self-criticism betrays him into errors of esthetics. Surely—and all that has little bearing on the fact that *Adventures of Huckleberry Finn* has a vigor, a depth, and a multiplicity which no other American novel surpasses, if in fact any equals them. It has the authority over the imagination which only great fiction can have.[26]

Twain deserves all of the credit for having written so fine a novel, but he must also shoulder some of the blame for the fact that so many readers have misread key features of Huck and Jim's crib. If blame is to be assigned, however, then serious "professional" readers must share some of it for failing to do even minimal research into the history of mid-nineteenth-century Mississippi River lumber, rafting, and steamboat culture.

How accurate are the many artistic depictions of the raft?

I began this chapter with the inauthentic cover illustration of a book called *Huck's Raft*. It shows a tiny raft made of small boards nailed over little logs. I close the chapter with reproductions of several more flawed cover illustrations. Most of these, unaccountably, also show the raft as a log raft with a top layer of boards rather than as a lumber raft. The various cover artists seem to have been influenced less by a careful reading of the novel than by a glance at the drawings of E. W. Kemble, who illustrated the first US edition (fig. 1.15).

Twain was not always pleased with Kemble's drawings. On May 24, 1884, having seen some of Kemble's illustrations for *Huckleberry Finn*, he wrote to his publisher, Charles Webster, that "much of the drawing in these pictures is careless and bad. The pictures will *do*—but they will just barely do—and that is the best I can say for them" (*HF* 375). He did not cite any particular problems with Kemble's portrayal of Huck and Jim's crib, but he can scarcely have been pleased with Kemble's failure to draw more accurately Huck and Jim's little section of a lumber raft. He must have been upset that Kemble drew a log raft rather than a lumber raft and that he showed Jim using a pole rather than the steering oars that Twain had described.

Following Kemble's lead, virtually all the illustrators of *Huckleberry Finn* have also depicted Huck and Jim's raft as a log raft rather than a lumber raft (figs. 1.16 through 1.24). The covers also show how profoundly misleading the various artists were in depicting other features of rafts and rafting, like the wigwam and the steering oars. Many of the cover illustrations show Huck and,

Figure 1.15. E. W. Kemble's first drawing of Huck and Jim's raft (*HF* 77). This drawing depicts a log raft, not a lumber raft, with the logs held together by a strip of wood (as in the log raft shown in figure 1.2). Kemble's drawing shows no pine planks or sweeps. It shows Jim with a push-pole and Huck with (apparently) a fishing pole. Twain makes no mention of either kind of pole in *Huckleberry Finn*.

especially, Jim using a push-pole to move the raft. Huck never mentions such poles, which would have been all but useless to Mississippi raftsmen. The raft had to be kept out in the main channel of the river, where the water would have been too deep for such poles.

We all know that you can't tell a book by its cover, but we also know that a cover can influence the way readers visualize the people, objects, and events in a book. It matters that virtually all the book-cover illustrators, with the exception of John Falter on the 1982 Macmillan cover, mislead readers by inviting them to imagine the raft as a self-contained log raft rather than what it was, a piece of a lumber raft.

I discuss steering oars and wigwams in the next chapter. For now, simply consider what the readers of the novel with such covers were led to imagine a steering oar and a wigwam to be. I do not mean to be unduly critical of the cover artists. They were, for the most part, underfed, underpaid, and under intense pressure to get the job done so the novel could be published. The editors who hired them to produce a cover would not have rewarded them to do historical research or to read the novel with special care—or, indeed, to read it at all.

Figure 1.16. Paul Laune's cover illustration for the undated Grossett and Dunlap edition. This drawing shows not a lumber raft but a log raft with planks fastened to the logs. It also shows Huck with a fishing pole and Jim with a push-pole. The wigwam is not raised above the surface of the raft, as it should be. The vertical boards on the wigwam, with no battens (small strips nailed over the cracks), would surely leak when it rained.

Figure 1.17. Cover of the undated Apple Classics edition. The unidentified cover artist shows a log raft with no plank surface. Huck is again shown with a fishing pole. Jim seems to be pushing on a cut sapling. The wigwam appears to be made of not of boards, as Twain said, but of canvas draped over sharpened saplings.

Figure 1.18. Cover of the 2014 Cozy Classics edition. Presumably one of the editors, Jack or Holman Wang, is the cover artist of this children's version of Huck's story. The log raft has a top layer of boards. There is only one steering oar (of sorts) and no wigwam.

Figure 1.19. Cover of the 2010 Classics Illustrated edition. The artist is not specified. Huck moves his boards-over-logs raft with a wooden pole, not a steering oar. No wigwam is in sight here, but the cartoons inside show a canvas tentlike enclosure. (*Classics Illustrated: The Adventures of Huckleberry Finn* © 2017 First Classics, Inc. By permission of Classic Comic Store Ltd.)

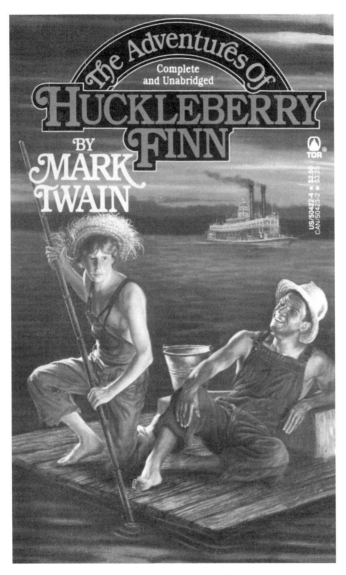

Figure 1.20. Cover of the 1985 Tom Doherty edition. The cover artist is not specified. Here Huck uses a bamboo push-pole, not a steering oar, and there is no wigwam—and no room for one—on the tiny raft, which seems to be made up of planks nailed onto floating logs.

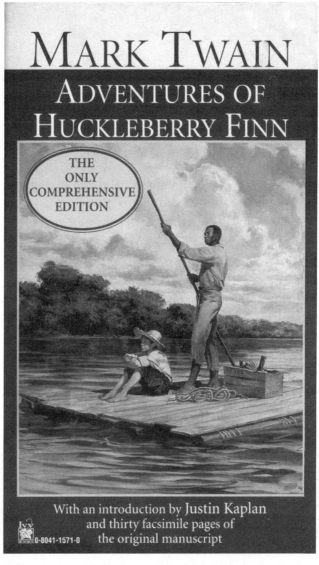

Figure 1.21. Cover of the 1997 Ivy Books edition. The artist is not specified. The raft is boards over logs and is therefore not a lumber raft. It has only a single steering oar—or is it a push-pole?—and no wigwam.

Figure 1.22. Cover of the 2014 Sheba Blake edition. No cover artist is mentioned. The raft is clearly a log raft with no pine-plank surface, no steering oars, and no Jim or wigwam in sight.

Figure 1.23. Cover of the undated Vintage Classics edition. No cover artist is mentioned. The raft shown here is made of tiny logs. There is no wigwam and no steering oar. The sitting Jim seems to be using a short pole to move the raft.

THE
ADVENTURES OF
HUCKLEBERRY FINN
by MARK TWAIN
illustrated by JOHN FALTER

with an afterword by CLIFTON FADIMAN

Figure 1.24. John Falter's cover illustration for the 1962 Macmillan edition. This is the only cover drawing I have seen that shows protruding grub stakes on what is pretty clearly a lumber raft. There are too many of the grub stakes to be realistic, but at least they are there. There is no center binder plank. The wigwam is raised above the surface, although the wigwam itself is not made of boards and looks more like a canvas pup tent than the one that Twain described. Jim uses a push-pole off the side, not a steering oar off the back, and there is no matching one at the front of the raft. Nevertheless, Falter is to be commended for doing some research on what a little segment of a lumber raft actually looked like. The heavy binder planks, the absence of a center binder plank, the snag in the river to the right, the use of a pole rather than a steering oar, and the whiskey jug all suggest that Falter was influenced by George Caleb Bingham's 1847 painting, *Raftsmen Playing Cards* (discussed in chapter 2).

CHAPTER TWO

"Right in the middle of the wigwam"

Shelter, Oars, Smallpox

A FEW DAYS AFTER Huck and Jim catch their little section of a lumber raft, Huck learns from Mrs. Loftus that certain townspeople are planning to search Jackson's Island, hoping to capture the runaway slave Jim. Huck quickly returns to the island and announces to Jim, "They're after us!" (*HF* 75). He is wrong, of course. They are after Jim, not "us," but Huck already feels a sense of kinship with the runaway slave. He and Jim hastily load their gear onto their crib and cast off. The next day Jim builds a wigwam on the raft and makes an extra steering oar. In this chapter I try to help readers of *Huckleberry Finn* answer several more questions: What was a wigwam? What was a steering oar? How was a steering oar different from a rudder? Why did Jim and Huck need to build an extra steering oar? What did Huck and Jim's little raft actually look like? Where did Twain get the idea for Huck's lie to the two fugitive-slave hunters in the skiff that the raft is infected with smallpox?

Careful readers might have inferred—correctly, of course—from Huck's use of "the top planks" in the following passage that there were more planks underneath:

> Jim took up some of **the top planks** of the raft and built a snug **wigwam** to get under in blazing weather and rainy, and to keep the things dry. Jim made a floor for the wigwam and raised it a foot or more above the level of the raft, so now the blankets and all the traps was out of reach of steamboat waves. Right in the middle of the **wigwam** we made a layer of dirt about five or six inches deep with a frame around it for to hold it to its place; this was to build a fire on in sloppy weather or chilly; the **wigwam** would keep it from being seen. (*HF* 78)

What was a wigwam?

Originally a wigwam was a domelike structure built by some Native American tribes to provide shelter. It typically consisted of large pieces of bark fastened over a framework of bent saplings. It was a temporary structure used for a while, then either abandoned or taken apart and moved elsewhere in pieces. In chapter 3 of *Life on the Mississippi* Twain looked back on the days of his youth:

> In the heyday of the steamboating prosperity, the river from end to end was flaked with coal-fleets and timber rafts, all managed by hand, and employing hosts of the rough characters whom I have been trying to describe. I remember the annual procession of mighty rafts that used to glide by Hannibal when I was a boy,—an acre or so of white, sweet-smelling boards in each raft, a crew of two dozen men or more, **three or four wigwams** scattered about the raft's vast level space for storm-quarters. (*LM* 239)

Similar to Native American wigwams, raft wigwams were temporary structures that were abandoned or dismantled when the raft reached its destination. We know only that Jim's wigwam is made of pine planks that he "took up" from the raft, that it is "snug," that it is raised a foot or more above the surface of the raft, and that it is large enough to sleep two men, house a raised cooking fire, and provide storage for straw and corn-shuck ticks, blankets, tools, and assorted other gear ("traps") that Huck and Jim had brought with them or had taken from the floating house—not to mention everything the king and the duke bring with them in their carpetbags. The wigwam might have been made by leaning vertical rows of planks against a horizontal pole, but that is unlikely. Unless the cracks between the boards were covered with wooden strips or battens nailed in place, such a roof would surely have leaked. A leaky roof would scarcely have been "snug" and would not have kept the men or their equipment dry. It is far more likely that Jim would have overlapped the planks horizontally to shed the water (fig. 2.1).

There are problems with Huck's description of the way Jim built the wigwam. Huck reports that Jim "took up some of the top planks" to do so. These would have been the top layer of twelve-foot-long planks. Those planks, however, would have been held securely in place by the three sixteen-foot binder planks above them. The only way to take up the twelve-footers would have been for Jim to remove the witch wedges in the grub stakes holding the binder

Figure 2.1. Three wigwams on a lumber raft. The wigwams here, like the one built by Jim, were set a foot off the surface of the raft to protect the occupants from waves. The slanted roof was made by overlapping horizontal boards. In these minimal-height wigwams, there was no possibility of an open fireplace. In the left foreground there is a yoke made of a lumber slab slipped down over two grub stakes. The yoke secured one crib to the one beside it. This etching and the next four were made from photographs taken by H. H. Bennett in 1886. (Courtesy of the McMillan Memorial Library, Wisconsin Rapids)

planks tight to the foundation planks. With the nine witches removed, the tension that held the whole crib together would have been lost, and the crib would have separated. Of course, if he had a witching lever and the right witching wedges, Jim might have been able to rewitch the raft at the nine grub stakes, but he had neither the witch tool nor the witch wedges. The only tools that Huck mentions are the "old rusty wood-saw without any handle" (*HF* 31) that he had found in the log shanty he shared with his pap, the "butcher knife without any handle and a bran-new Barlow knife," and the "hatchet and some nails" (*HF* 62) that he and Jim found in the floating house. Jim could have used that saw to cut each of the twelve-foot planks in two after they had been removed from the raft. And he could have used the hatchet and nails to fasten the six-foot boards together to build the wigwam, but these tools would not have helped to resecure the binder planks after the twelve-footers had been taken up.

It would seem, then, that Twain's knowledge of how lumber cribs were actually constructed was limited. He apparently knew little about what held them together and what would happen if they were taken apart before they reached their destination. Had he known, he would have had Jim build the wigwam out of some other boards—such as floating planks he fished out of the river.

Another problem with Huck and Jim's wigwam is that Twain put a fireplace inside it. A raised and unvented open fire "right in the middle" of a "snug" low-roofed structure would have been both smoky and hazardous, especially adjacent to the highly inflammable "straw tick" and the "corn-shuck tick" that were kept in the wigwam (HF 167).

Still another problem with the large wigwam that Twain described was that it would have acted as a sail, catching the wind and blowing the little raft around. Even on the huge rafts, Walter A. Blair says, the raftsmen were forced to sleep in very low structures. Blair called the structures tents and shanties rather than wigwams:

> There was so much objection to any structure that would catch wind and cause more work at the oars, that they were contented with very small tents made of rough boards. If any ambitious members of the crew built higher shanties they were usually told to knock them down, the first windy day. Failure to comply with this suggestion frequently resulted in a fight that was sure to end in defeat for the owner, because the pilot or the rest of the crew would knock it down anyway.[1]

If a huge, heavy raft was susceptible to being blown about by the wind, Huck and Jim's little crib would have been even more susceptible. It is therefore curious that Huck and Jim's crib, with its prominent wigwam acting as a sail, does not appear to be blown about much by the wind on the night of the terrible storm in chapter 20: "it come on to rain and blow and thunder and lighten like everything. . . . My souls, how the wind did scream along! . . . you'd see . . . the trees thrashing around in the wind" (HF 167–68). Huck mentions the wind blowing the trees, and he mentions the waves knocking the raft around, but he does not mention the wind directly moving the raft. Nor does he mention that the wigwam in which the king and the duke sleep is causing the raft to be pushed away from its designated position in "the middle of the river" (*HF* 167).

The wigwam on Huck and Jim's raft must be sizable. Assuming that it is six feet long and big enough to have a fireplace, to sleep the king and the duke, and to store all the equipment that the four have with them, it must be at least five feet wide and five feet high. The wigwam would have dominated the crib, taking up fully one-sixth of the surface. It would leave little space for the two steering oars.

From his vantage point at the head of Jackson's Island the morning after he escapes from his pap, Huck hears a voice from the big lumber raft saying, "**Stern oars**, there!—heave her head to stabboard!" (*HF* 44). What Huck hears is the voice of the raft pilot telling the raftsmen manning the sweeps at the back of the raft to push their large steering oars so that the rear of the raft will swing left, thus making the front of the raft swing right, or starboard.

What was a steering oar?

A steering oar, often called a sweep, was a long oar that pivoted on a vertical pin at the front or rear edge of a raft. An oarsman moved the wet end of the sweep in or out of the water on that pivot pin, which served as a kind of oarlock. He pushed the steering oar back and forth by walking in an arc on the deck (figure 1.2 showed a good close-up of a sweep). The sweeps were designed not to propel the raft down the river but to move it short distances sideways to keep it in the middle of the channel; to keep it from hitting rocks, trees, snags, riverbanks, or other river traffic; and to keep it from floating sideways down the river. The oars could be of various lengths, depending on the size of the raft and the strength, size, and experience of the raftsmen. The steering oars on a big Wisconsin or Mississippi raft or a single-string rapids piece would have been long and heavy. Blair described them as follows:

> The oars or sweeps by which the raft was handled consisted of stems twenty feet long, usually young tamarack poles, about twelve inches thick at the big end. Into this was pinned a pine blade fourteen inches wide, about twelve feet long, and two and one-half inches thick at the end attached to the [stem] and sawed tapering to one and one-quarter inches at the outboard end.[2]

With a twenty-foot stem attached to a twelve-foot blade, the oar was thirty feet long, assuming a two-foot overlap. That jibes well enough with Robert Fries's observation:

> Until the mid-sixties all rafts were floated downriver by the current and kept in the channel by crews who managed them at bow and stern with sweeps about thirty feet long. Pulling a raft oar required skill and great strength. The operator dipped the oar by swinging it at arm's length above his head and then, walking in a short arc, surging upon it at each step until the stroke was completed.[3]

It was, of course, hard work to move a heavy raft with a heavy steering oar (figs. 2.2 through 2.5).

Figure 2.2. A raftsman pushes on his steering oar. Notice the size of the log from which the oar was made, and imagine the strength it would have taken to move the raft sideways with such an oar. The end of the oar has been shaved to make it easier for the raftsman to grasp it. Notice the wigwam to the left of the raftsman and, beyond that, another raftsman steering the other end of the raft. Notice also the bundles of wood strips, which are probably to be sold as plaster laths. Just beyond the near raftsman's boots is the joint between two cribs, and to the left of the wigwam is a series of yokes. This raft is apparently three strings wide and five cribs long. The cribs to the left are apparently only eight feet wide. (Courtesy of the McMillan Memorial Library, Wisconsin Rapids)

Figure 2.3. Three raftsmen lift a heavy steering oar onto the grub stake that is to serve as its oarlock or pivot pin. Notice the rounded headblock at the base of the grub stake, which is used to hold the steering oar higher. (Courtesy of the McMillan Memorial Library, Wisconsin Rapids)

Figure 2.4. A raftsman walks the planks to steer his end of the lumber raft. His steering oar pivots on a grub stake that is anchored by a strip of wood to the one to its left to keep it from bending or breaking off from the tremendous force of the oar in the water. The coil of rope would have been used to stop ("check" or "snub") the raft. One end would have been tied to a tree on the riverbank, the other to the raft. (Courtesy of the McMillan Memorial Library, Wisconsin Rapids)

Figure 2.5. A raftsman reaches high to make sure the other end of the steering oar is deep enough in the water to let him move that end of the raft. To make it possible for him to push the wet end even deeper, he has made himself a raised walkway. Just behind that are several yokes slipped down over the grub stakes to hold one string of cribs to the adjacent string. Behind the stretching raftsman in the picture (i.e., to his left) is the sheltered area that served as a kitchen and dining area for the crew. It has no sides so that the raft will not be pushed around by the wind. (Courtesy of the McMillan Memorial Library, Wisconsin Rapids)

Malcolm Rosholt gave a somewhat different and more detailed description of the steering oars:

> Rafts were guided by long oars, forty-five to fifty feet long. The oars were made of planks sixteen feet long coupled to a long, heavy pole smoothed off at one end for easier handling. The oar was balanced at the bow and stern of the rapids-piece on a timber, called the "headblock," which was six by eight inches in thickness. The headblock was wedged securely into the raft by grubstakes, and a grubstake in the center of the headblock acted as oar lock. The men handling the oars at the stern of the rapids-piece were called "tailsmen," and the men up front, "bowsmen."[4]

Glover emphasized that the steering oars were designed merely to steer, not to propel, the raft:

> These **oars** swung directly to the front and rear, and were used only for steering. They were from thirty-six to fifty feet long; they apparently were lengthened with the experience of raftsmen. The blade was a carefully trimmed plank twelve to eighteen feet long mounted on a heavy pole which was smoothly finished for the oarsman's grasp. It was nicely balanced on the oar-pin.[5]

The oar pin was the center front or rear two-inch grub stake that served double duty. First, it served to hold the planks together by means of tight wedges. Second, especially if it were longer than the other grub stakes, it served as a vertical pivot for the steering oar, which had a two-inch hole drilled at or near its midpoint. The hole was chiseled slightly wider at the top and bottom front and rear to permit the oar, when lifted onto the grub stake, to pivot up and down. When the steersman pushed his end of the steering oar down, the wet end of the oar came out of the water so he could reposition it. When he pushed his end up, the wet end of the steering oar plunged back down into the water, so that by walking the other end along the deck he could move the end of the raft right or left in the water.

E. W. Kemble's illustration for chapter 20 (fig. 2.6) mistakenly shows Jim using a pole and Huck using a sweep as a rudder. Twain made no mention of a pole as a tool for moving the raft, and Huck could not have used a steering oar as a rudder.

Figure 2.6. Another drawing by E. W. Kemble of Huck and Jim's raft (*HF* 168). This drawing shows a log raft with a wigwam, complete with the feet of the sleeping king and duke. It does not show the wigwam as being raised "a foot or more above the level of the raft" (*HF* 78), and Kemble was ambiguous about the composition of the outer surface of the structure. He made it look more like a canvas pup tent than the wooden structure that Huck describes. The drawing shows Huck manning a single bent-handled sweep loosely held between two upright pegs, but Huck uses it as a rudder, not as part of a pair of sweeps. The drawing shows Jim at the side of the raft using a push-pole rather than opposite Huck at the forward end of the crib manning the other sweep. Huck never mentions a pole being used to move the raft.

What is the difference between a steering oar and a rudder?

It is easy to confuse a steering oar and a rudder. Both were flat, vertically oriented devices usually made of wood and placed in the water to control the movement of rivercraft. They were, however, really quite different. A rudder was a finlike board that stayed submerged in the water at the rear of a boat that had its own source of locomotion—usually wind, a steam engine, a tow rope, oars, or paddles. A sailboat was driven by the wind but was steered by its rudder. A steamboat had a rudder, although a side-wheel steamboat could also be steered by powering one side wheel faster than the other. A racing crew boat was powered by oars but was steered by a helmsman who operated the rudder at the very rear of the boat. A skiff, or rowboat, usually had no rudder because it was both powered and steered by oars. A canoe paddle powered the canoe forward and, when held steady in the water at the rear of the canoe, doubled as a temporary rudder to steer the canoe for a few feet before the paddle was pulled out and used again to propel the canoe forward.

A rudder would have been useless for steering a rivercraft that was not moving relative to the water it was immersed in. A sailboat on a river on a windless day could drift with the current but could not be steered by its rudder. The rudder on a becalmed sailboat could not change the direction of the boat, because the boat was stationary relative to the water surrounding it. A raft was like that becalmed sailboat. It had no source of locomotion except the river current that carried it along. A rudder would have been useless unless the raft was being moved faster than the surrounding current—unless, for example, it was being towed or pushed by a steamboat. If it were being towed or pushed by a steamboat, however, the steamboat would have directed the movement of the raft, and no rudder would have been necessary on the raft.

A Mississippi raft in the period we are speaking of—around the 1840s—was moved almost exclusively by the river current. The raft moved relative to the riverbank but not relative to the river current that pushed it along. To understand what I mean, imagine yourself as Huck in Kemble's drawing in the immediately preceding figure. Imagine that you see two logs, one stuck in the mud on the nearby riverbank and one floating in the river beside your raft. Ten minutes later the log on the riverbank will be long out of sight behind you, but the one in the water beside you will still be beside you, carried along by the same current that carries you. A rudder, then, could steer a rivercraft that had its own power but would have been useless to you on a raft that was drifting with the current.

It was very much in the interest of the raftsmen moving lumber downstream to market that the raft stay in the main channel of the river. To drift to one side or the other would not only slow the raft down but would endanger it. If it bumped into the riverbank or ran aground on a sandbar, the journey would be delayed even more. Furthermore, the raft might be damaged. The only auxiliary source of locomotion on a raft was provided by the steering oars (sweeps) on pivots at the front and rear of the raft. These steering oars were operated by strong men who dipped the steering oars into and out of the water and pushed them side to side. Their steering oars were emphatically not rudders. Unlike rudders, oars did not stay in the water but were tilted into and out of the water by the men. Their activities could better be described as reorienting the raft than as propelling it.

Immediately after his discussion of Jim's building of the wigwam, Huck mentions the steering oars that apparently were already part of the crib they had caught: "We made an **extra steering oar**, too, because one of the others might get broke, on a snag or something" (*HF* 78). The steering oars on Huck and Jim's small raft would have been far shorter than those thirty- to fifty-foot ones described by Blair, Fries, and Rosholt. Huck and Jim's crib is only sixteen feet long. Assuming that the wigwam would take at least five feet of that sixteen feet, the sweeps could not be much longer than ten feet, with five feet on either side of the pivot hole. In other words, if each oar had about five feet in the water and five on the crib, that would be adequate to steer so small a raft. The short sweeps would pivot on the center front and rear grub stakes.

What are the implications of that extra steering oar?

A raft needed two steering oars, or sweeps: one at the front and one at the rear. The sweeps were designed to work as a coordinated pair. Operating only one sweep would simply spin the raft—like rowing a boat with only one oar. That Jim and Huck made an extra steering oar because "**one of the others** might get broke, on a snag or something," proves that there were already two steering oars on their crib. That probably meant that this crib had been released from its parent rapids piece so it could run a particularly rough slide or rapids but that it had somehow dumped its oarsmen and floated downriver unmanned. If it already had two steering oars, why did Jim and Huck need to make an extra oar? After all, their plan is to sell the raft as soon as they get to Cairo and use the proceeds to pay for steamboat passage up the Ohio to the free states. They would know, however, that steering oars sometimes got lost or damaged.

In *Life on the Mississippi* Twain had mentioned a steamboat that destroyed steering oars on floating rivercraft:

> Then for an instant, as we whistled by, the red glare from our furnaces would reveal the scow and the form of the gesticulating orator as if under a lightning-flash, and in that instant our firemen and deck-hands would send and receive a tempest of missiles and profanity, one of our wheels would walk off with the crashing fragments of a steering-oar, and down the dead blackness would shut again. . . . Once a coal-boatman sent a bullet through our pilot-house, when we borrowed a steering-oar of him in a very narrow place. (*LM* 290–91)

If Huck and Jim lost a steering oar in such a collision, they would have had no way to land the raft at Cairo. It turns out that they were wise to make the spare steering oar, because one of the original oars does indeed get destroyed the night Jim and Huck are separated in the fog:

> When I got to it [the raft] Jim was setting there with his head down between his knees, asleep, with his right arm hanging over the **steering-oar**. The **other oar** was smashed off, and the raft was littered up with leaves and branches and dirt. So she'd had a rough time. (*HF* 102)

A rough time, indeed. With Huck gone there was no way for Jim to direct the movement of the raft. Making the spare steering oar shows that they knew that a raft with only one oar, or only one oarsman, could not be steered. They have a spare the night of the fog, but it is useless without Huck there to use it (figs. 2.7 and 2.8). An unsteerable raft would go wherever the current took it—under low branches, into rocks, or onto islands and riverbanks. A seven-ton piece of a lumber raft would have been particularly difficult for one oarsman to try to control, even if it were not enveloped in fog.

Huck and Jim understand that they are both needed to steer the raft. In describing the night of the storm, Huck says, "**We** didn't have no trouble about snags; the lightning was glaring and flittering around so constant that **we** could see them plenty soon enough to throw her head this way or that and miss them" (*HF* 168). Only after the storm dies down does Huck go to sleep while Jim takes the watch. Then Huck takes the watch while Jim sleeps. During those sleep times the raft is not steered. When dawn comes, however, Huck wakes

Figure 2.7. Kemble's drawing of Jim dozing with his arm over a steering oar (*HF* 102). There would have been no point in Jim's trying to steer the crib with only one steering oar and one oarsman. And with that kind of oarlock—two vertical pins with the oar not attached to either—the oar could easily have slipped away.

Figure 2.8. Kemble's drawing of Huck talking to Jim in the water (*HF* 128). Like the previous drawing, this one gets the oarlock wrong and does not secure the oar. These three illustrations by Kemble suggest that he thought the steering oar was a rudder. It was not.

Jim up so together they can steer the raft to shore: "I rousted him out and **we slid the raft into hiding quarters for the day**" (*HF* 168).

In chapter 16 the raftsmen on the big lumber raft are deployed in balanced sets: "just then there was a loud order to stand by for a crossing, and **some of them went forward** to man the sweeps there, and **the rest went aft** to handle the after-sweeps" (*HF* 111). In chapter 13 of *The Adventures of Tom Sawyer*, Twain had described the way the pretend pirates moved the little log raft they had just seized:

> They shoved off, presently, Tom in command, **Huck at the after oar** and **Joe at the forward**. Tom stood amidships, gloomy-browed, and with folded arms, and gave his orders in a low, stern whisper. . . . the boys steadily and monotonously drove the raft toward mid-stream. . . . The raft drew beyond the middle of the river; the boys pointed her head right, and then lay on their oars. (*TS* 88–89)

In neither novel did Twain ever speak of just one steering oar being used or of a steering oar being used as a rudder. The only time Huck tries to move the raft by himself is in chapter 31 of *Huckleberry Finn*. Huck has just learned that the king has sold Jim to Silas Phelps. Huck knows, then, that Jim cannot help him move the raft: "So then I took the bearings of a woody island that was down the river a piece, and as soon as it was fairly dark I crept out with my raft and went for it, and hid it there" (*HF* 271). Twain was noticeably vague here about *how* Huck "went for it." He did not say anything about Huck's using the steering oars. Twain knew that it would have been futile to try to move the raft with only one oarsman. Perhaps he wanted us to imagine that Huck towed the raft with his canoe.

Thomas Hart Benton, a later illustrator of *Huckleberry Finn*, criticized the work of his predecessor, E. W. Kemble, mostly on the grounds that as a New Englander, Kemble had never seen the Mississippi. Benton, in contrast, was a native Missourian and so could be more accurate in visually portraying the great novel:

> Certainly he [Kemble] made no special research into the physical conditions of the story's setting. He undertook the job with no first-hand knowledge of the great river and its country. He knew nothing about the people along the river. He drew his Mississippi characters, with few exceptions, like Connecticut Yankees.

This was all right for the King and the Duke, for these were carpet-bag characters down south before their historic time; but to find the boatmen of the great river and the town-loafers of its banks looking like New England rock-grubbers is something of a shock. . . . I know the river, and its backwaters and tributaries, not only as geographical facts but as waters over which the sun rises and sets and casts reflections, pink and blue and red and black. I was raised among people who talked the language of Huck Finn's people, who thought like them, and acted like them. I am in that book just as the book, after all these years of reading it, is in me.[6]

Benton's illustrations of Huck and Jim's raft, however, show that he knew little more than Kemble did about what the raft looked like. He got the wigwam more or less right in his illustration for the book version (fig. 2.9). He got it all wrong, however, in the mural he painted at the Missouri State Museum (not shown here). In both, the raft that he depicted is a log raft, not a lumber raft, and it has only one steering oar, which is being used as a rudder.

Figure 2.9. Thomas Hart Benton's 1942 illustration of Huck and Jim's raft as it approaches the wreck of the *Walter Scott* in chapter 12. Benton got the wigwam more or less right, but he placed it on a log raft with a top layer of planks, not on a lumber raft. He put a small fireplace just outside the wigwam, not in the middle of it where Twain put it. Benton did not show the wigwam raised a foot above the surface of the raft, and he placed the wigwam at the very front of the raft, right where the fore steering oar would have to have been. (Image reprinted with the permission of MBI Inc.)

Cover artists, often following Kemble's misleading example, have made many misrepresentations of the wigwam and the steering oars on Huck and Jim's raft (figs. 2.12 through 2.21 on pages 76–85).

I want to consider one more artist's rendering of a lumber raft. Unlike the others we have been considering, this one was not meant to be a cover illustration for *Huckleberry Finn*. Indeed, it precedes Twain's novel by more than thirty years. George Caleb Bingham (1811–1897) was born in Virginia but soon moved, with his parents and siblings, to Missouri. He apprenticed himself there to a cabinetmaker, but soon he discovered that his real vocation was painting. He lived most of his life in the vicinity of both the Missouri and the Mississippi Rivers. His most famous paintings—*Fur Traders Descending the Missouri* (1845) and *The Jolly Flatboatmen* (1846)—both have river settings. My interest here, however, is in a less famous painting, also with a river setting: *Raftsmen Playing Cards* (1847).

The first thing to notice about *Raftsmen Playing Cards* (fig. 2.10) is that the raft is a lumber raft held together by grub stakes—the vertical posts that stick up above the binder planks and go clear through to the parallel foundation planks (underwater and thus not visible in the painting) at the bottom of the raft. Most lumber rafts, as we have seen, had a third binder plank running down the center of the raft, but the raft in the Bingham painting does not. The raft itself appears to be the front end of a rapids piece—that is, a long, narrow stringing together of several cribs. It is impossible to determine from this painting how many cribs are on the rapids piece. Indeed, the large number of raftsmen—six are in full view—would have been unusual on a rapids piece, which could manage easily with half that number. The apparent narrowness of the river ahead of the raft suggests that because there may be more rapids ahead, the rapids piece has not yet been yoked at the side to other rapids pieces to make up a Wisconsin raft. The fact that the raftsman at the back of the picture (which is the front of the raft) is using a push-pole rather than a steering oar, or sweep, suggests that the river here is not deep. That interpretation is corroborated by the appearance of a snag—apparently a limb from a submerged tree—to the right and ahead of the raft, and by the presence of a sandbar just ahead and to the left of the raft. Indeed, the raftsman with the pole may be attempting to push the raft away from the sandbar.

There is apparently some sort of stack or structure behind the card players. It is possibly a wigwam, although we cannot say for sure. Whatever it is, it and

Figure 2.10. George Caleb Bingham's *Raftsmen Playing Cards* (1847). This painting by an artist who lived near the Mississippi and Missouri Rivers at about the time Twain's *Huckleberry Finn* is set shows what the fore end of a rapids piece looked like. Note particularly the grub stakes and, in the shadowed foreground, the raised earth-filled fire bed. The raftsmen are passing the time with a game of cards while their raft drifts slowly downstream. Perhaps before long they will be called to man the sweeps (not shown) when the next rapids or crossing comes into view. (George Caleb Bingham, American, 1811–1897; *Raftsmen Playing Cards*, 1847; oil on canvas, approximately 28 x 38 inches; Saint Louis Art Museum, bequest of Ezra H. Linley by exchange 50:1934)

the raftsmen themselves block our view of the fore steering oar that would have been there. If there is a wigwam there, it probably did not have a fireplace inside, to judge from the existence of a raised fireplace box filled with dirt in the shadowed center foreground of the painting and from the scraps of kindling and firewood scattered about right next to it. The loose diagonal plank sticking out to the right was apparently to be used as a gangplank to permit the men to walk ashore when the raft was tied up for the night. The presence of the jug at the left suggests that these raftsmen, like the ones on the huge raft in chapter 16 of *Huckleberry Finn*, enjoyed a spot of whiskey from time to time.

Twain announced on the title page of *Adventures of Huckleberry Finn* that the novel is set "Forty to Fifty Years Ago" (*HF* vii), which is usually taken to mean between 1835 and 1845. Because Bingham is generally assumed to have based his paintings on his own observations of river life, a painting of a section of a lumber raft dated just after the announced period covered by the novel is of special interest. Had Kemble and later illustrators consulted *Raftsmen Playing Cards*, they might have been guided by some of its features. With the possible exception of John Falter (whose illustration was shown in figure 1.24), they apparently did not consult it.

So if virtually all previous artistic renderings of Huck and Jim's raft are wrong, what, if anything, was right?

What did Huck and Jim's crib, wigwam, and steering oars probably look like?

To give a sense of the proportions of Huck and Jim's crib, I provide here a scale drawing (fig. 2.11) of a twelve-foot by sixteen-foot lumber crib with a two-man wigwam. Tethered to the raft is a fourteen-foot birchbark canoe.

It is on just such a raft, and in just such a canoe, that Huck plays out his struggle with his conscience at the end of chapter 16. Eager to be free, Jim begins to think that every light he sees is Cairo: "Dah she is! . . . Dah's Cairo!" (*HF* 123–24). Suddenly realizing that Jim might soon be free, Huck is stricken

Figure 2.11. A reasonable depiction of Jim and Huck's crib, by Calloway M'Cloud and Bill Curr.

by pangs of "conscience" because he had helped Jim escape from his "rightful owner," Miss Watson:

> It hadn't ever come home to me before what this thing was that I was doing. But now it did; and it staid with me, and scorched me more and more. I tried to make out to myself that I warn't to blame, because I didn't run Jim off from his rightful owner; but it warn't no use, conscience up and says, every time, "But you knowed he was running for his freedom and you could a paddled ashore and told somebody." (*HF* 123–24)

When he hears Jim talk about coming back someday to steal his children, Huck feels even more guilty:

> It most froze me to hear such talk. . . .
> I was sorry to hear Jim say that, it was such a lowering of him. My conscience got to stirring me up hotter than ever, until at last I says to it, "Let up on me—it ain't too late, yet—I'll paddle ashore at the first light and tell." (*HF* 124)

Huck's conscience transforms the raft from what has been a safe haven for Jim up to that point as he runs for freedom into a place of danger where Jim is trapped, not knowing that Huck intends to tell the authorities that they will find a runaway slave on the raft. And Huck's conscience transforms the canoe as well. Up to that point it has been a means for him and Jim to make their escape up the Ohio River to freedom, but now it has become a means of betrayal.

When Jim sees a light up ahead, he is convinced that it is Cairo: "We's safe, Huck, we's safe! Jump up and crack yo' heels, dat's de good ole Cairo at las' I jis' knows it!" (*HF* 124). Seeing his chance to turn Jim in, Huck tells Jim that he will take the canoe and go find out if the light is indeed Cairo.

Almost immediately Huck is given the chance to report Jim. When he is only fifty yards away from the raft, two men with guns approach his canoe in a skiff. One of them questions Huck:

> "What's that yonder?"
> "A piece of a raft," I says.
> "Do you belong on it?"
> "Yes, sir."
> "Any men on it?"

"Only one, sir."

"Well, there's five niggers run off, to-night, up yonder above the head of the bend. Is your man white or black?" (*HF* 125)

Here is Huck's chance to salve his "conscience." All he has to do is tell the truth and say "black." But he cannot do it:

I didn't answer up prompt. I tried to, but the words wouldn't come. I tried, for a second or two, to brace up, and out with it, but I warn't man enough—hadn't the spunk of a rabbit. I see I was weakening; so I just give up trying, and up and says—

"He's white."

"I reckon we'll go and see for ourselves." (*HF* 125)

Then, having told one lie, Huck quickly follows up with several more:

"I wish you would," says I, "because it's pap that's there, and maybe you'd help me tow the raft ashore where the light is. He's sick—and so is mam and Mary Ann."

"Oh, the devil! We're in a hurry, boy. But I s'pose we've got to. Come—buckle to your paddle, and let's get along."

I buckled to my paddle and they laid to their oars. When we had made a stroke or two, I says:

"Pap'll be mighty much obleeged to you, I can tell you. Everybody goes away when I want them to help me tow the raft ashore, and I can't do it by myself."

"Well, that's infernal mean. Odd, too. Say, boy, what's the matter with your father?"

"It's the—a—the—well, it ain't anything, much." (*HF* 125–26)

From Huck's clever lies the slave hunters conclude that Huck's father, mother, and sister all have smallpox. They immediately back their skiff away, and Jim is safe.

It is an important scene for Huck. He begins it determined to turn Jim in by telling the truth: that the man on the raft is a black runaway slave. He ends it determined to save Jim by telling a lie: that the man on the raft is a white man with smallpox. For the greedy slave hunters, Huck's lies transform the raft from a place they can make some easy money by capturing a fugitive slave to a place of contagion.

Where did Twain get the idea for Huck's lie about smallpox?

There has been some speculation about where Twain got the idea for Huck's smallpox lie. One scholar thought that Twain borrowed the idea from Harriet Beecher Stowe's story "Captain Kidd's Money," in *Sam Lawson's Oldtown Fireside Stories* (1871), about a woman (Mother Hokum) who owes the butcher (Joe Gidger) two dollars. When Joe comes to collect the money, she tells him that her husband (Hokum) has smallpox:

> Mother Hokum she see him a comin' jest as he come past the juniper-bush on the corner. She says to Hokum, "Get into bed old man, quick, and let me tell the story," says she. So she covered him up; and when Gidger come in she come up to him, and says she, "Why, Mr. Gidger, I'm jest ashamed to see ye: why, Mr. Hokum was jest a comin' down to pay ye that 'are money last week, but ye see he was took down with the small-pox"—Joe didn't hear no more; he just turned round, and he streaked it out of that 'are door with his coat-tails flyin' straight out ahind him; and old Mother Hokum she jest stood there at the window holdin' her sides and laughin' fit to split, to see him run.[7]

Another scholar suggested that Twain took the idea from James Pennington's slave narrative, *The Fugitive Blacksmith* (1850). Pennington was a slave who had run away from his owner's plantation in Maryland and headed for Philadelphia. He did not get very far before he was captured by some Maryland farmers who asked him whom he belonged to and where he came from. Knowing that to tell the truth would mean being sold to a Louisiana plantation owner, Pennington decided to tell the lie that he was a free man. The farmers were skeptical and said they would put him in jail overnight and take him to a magistrate in the morning. Pennington said that if they would not put him in jail he would tell them the truth about where he was from. When they agreed, he told them another lie:

> "Well," said I, "a few weeks ago, I was sold from the eastern shore to a slave-trader, who had a large gang, and set out for Georgia, but when he got to a town in

Virginia, he was taken sick, and died with the small-pox. Several of his gang also died with it, so that the people in the town became alarmed, and did not wish the gang to remain among them. No one claimed us, or wished to have anything to do with us; I left the rest, and thought I would go somewhere and get work."[8]

Pennington never directly said that he himself had smallpox, but his lie led his captors to think that he did. It had the desired effect of sending most of his accusers home immediately. They wanted to have nothing to do with a man who had been near others who had smallpox. They left him under the guard of one of the white men. The next morning Pennington easily outran his guard and made his escape.

In neither of these possible sources, however, is there a river or a raft. A more likely origin for Huck's smallpox lie can be found in a supposedly true story referred to in the memoirs of former Mississippi raft pilot Walter A. Blair. Regarding the meals provided to raftsmen, he stated the following:

The conveniences of life were very meager, but the work was healthful, and the life, and excitement, in the open pure air gave them good appetites and excellent digestion. They usually had plenty of good plain food, and strong coffee. They seldom had any ice, in the hottest weather, or any milk. Sometimes, delayed on a long hard trip, when the pilot's money or credit gave out, these men were just as resourceful as any of General Sherman's soldiers on their March to the Sea.

The country above Dubuque was very sparsely settled, and the little towns far apart, but it is pleasant to reflect that there is no record of a raftman dying of hunger. An angry farmer, who missed a fat two-year-old heifer one morning after a raft had passed down, overtook the raft by a long, hard row in a heavy skiff. The dressed carcass lay on the logs near the center of the raft, covered with a piece of white canvas. The crew was divided and crouched at the corners of the raft, while the old French pilot sat alone with his head down, when the farmer appeared and questioned him. Old George said, "My friend, I'm glad to see you. I'm in big trouble. My crew are all afraid of me." "How so?" "You see," he replied, "that white ting down there?—small pox, one of my best men, the cook. I stay and work with him all night but 'taint no use. Now, my friend, you look like a brave man. I want you to help me take the cook ashore and bury him." But the farmer was gone; nearly fell in the river in his excitement and hurry to get away.[9]

Twain, of course, could not have read Blair's memoirs, which were published in 1930, but he might have heard the story of the raft pilot's smallpox lie. It was just the kind of story that pilots, steamboat crews, and raftsmen would enjoy telling and retelling around the stove or fireplace during leisure hours up and down the Mississippi River. Unlike the other two suggested sources, this one involves a raft on the Mississippi, a suspicious man in a skiff, a lament that others have refused to help, a specious request that the man in the skiff help in getting the raft with its infected cargo ashore, and his hasty retreat from the raft. The similarities with Huck's smallpox lie may, of course, be coincidental, but the parallels make Blair's narrative a more likely source than the other two.

It is interesting that Huck's smallpox lie involves not only a raft and a skiff but a canoe as well. Huck's conscience cannot let him transform the raft, the site of Jim's run for freedom, into the site of Jim's capture. Whatever the source of the idea for Huck's smallpox lie, Twain adapted it brilliantly to showcase the raft, the skiff, and the canoe as the three-rivercraft setting for what is arguably the most important scene in the novel, Huck's struggle with his "conscience" about freedom and slavery, right and wrong, good and bad, love and greed, loyalty and disloyalty, and truth and falsehood.

Canoes, skiffs, and other Mississippi rivercraft are the subjects of the next chapter.

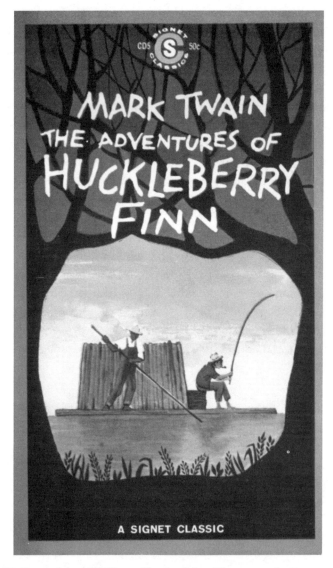

Figure 2.12. Cover of the 1959 Signet Classic edition. The cover artist is not named. The composition of the raft is not clear, but Jim is using a pole, not a steering oar, and Huck is fishing with a fishing pole, not a trotline. The wigwam, made of vertical boards, dominates the small raft.

Figure 2.13. Tom Lowell's cover illustration for the 1981 Bantam Classic edition. The raft is made of logs with a top deck of boards, it has only a single steering oar, and the wigwam is a not-so-snug lean-to.

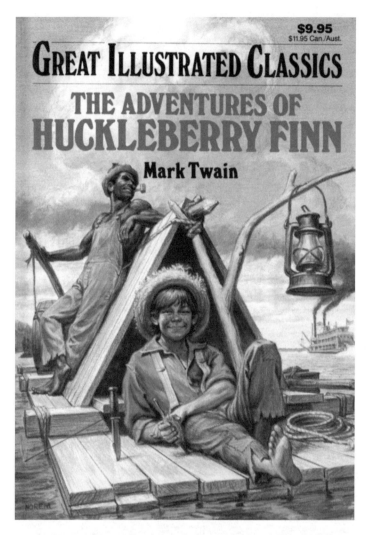

Figure 2.14. Earl Norem's cover illustration for the 1990 Great Illustrated Classics edition. Norem depicts a lumber raft, although he shows the lumber held together by ropes, not grub stakes, and stacked parallel, not crisscrossed. The wigwam here is made of boards with a raised floor, but the vertical roof boards would surely have leaked. Jim is shown with his hand casually holding what is apparently a rudder or tiller. Nothing resembling a steering oar is in sight. The knife stuck in the board is more like a World War II army-issue knife than the folding Barlow pocketknife Huck is said to have. The illustrations for the inside of the book were done by a different (and unnamed) artist. There the drawings show a different—and even less accurate—raft.

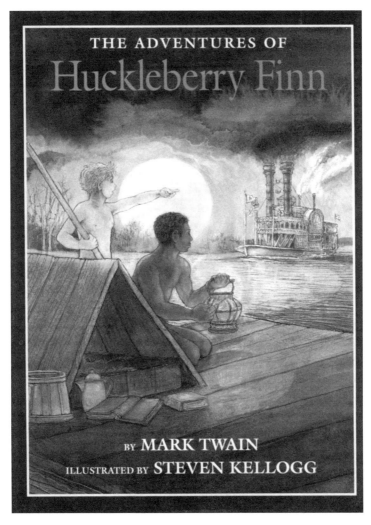

Figure 2.15. Steven Kellogg's cover illustration for the 1994 William Morrow edition. The full nudity of Huck and Jim is concealed behind the wigwam, which is appropriately raised above the surface of the raft. The vertical board roof would leak, however. The raft itself has a board surface, but it is not clear what is under the top layer—logs or more lumber. If the drawing is meant to show the raft about to be struck by the steamboat, it is curious that the artist shows no steering oars that might permit Huck and Jim to move the raft out of its path. A drawing inside the book (facing page 98) shows a raft with a single rudder, not a pair of steering oars.

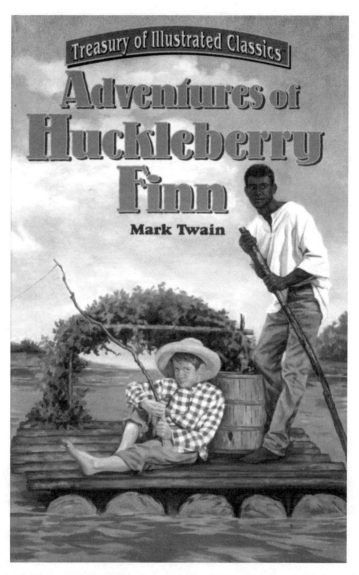

Figure 2.16. Richard Lauter's cover illustration for the 1999 Modern Publishing edition. The raft shown is a log raft, not a lumber raft; Jim is using a pole, not a steering oar; and Huck is fishing with a fishing pole, not the trotline he is said to use. Most curious of all is the depiction of the wigwam as a leafy archway or bower.

Figure 2.17. Kenny McKendry's cover illustration for the 1995 Cambridge University Press edition. The raft appears to be a lumber raft, but the top boards are nailed to whatever is underneath, thus ruining the lumber for sale as building material. Huck appears to be using the pole as a rudder, and it has no mate at the front end of the raft. The wigwam appears to be made of canvas and is not raised above the surface of the raft.

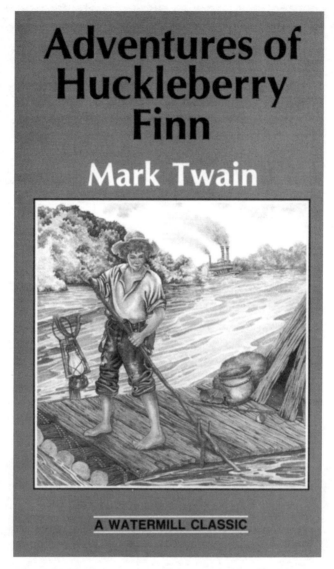

Figure 2.18. Pat and Robin DeWitt's cover illustration for the 1998 Watermill Classic edition. Almost everything is wrong with this rendition: it depicts a log raft, not a lumber raft; the steering oar is too skinny; it comes off the side rather than the end of the raft, and there is only one; the wigwam is not raised; and the boards are vertical and thus leaky.

Figure 2.19. Dan Andreasen's cover illustration for the 2006 Classic Starts Sterling Children's Books edition. It is not clear what the top planks are fastened to or how they are fastened. There is a pole instead of a steering oar. The wigwam looks like an outhouse.

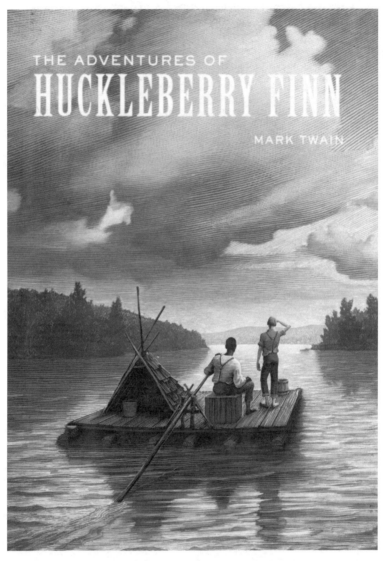

Figure 2.20. Scott McKowen's cover illustration for the 2006 edition (no publisher given). The logs are beneath the top layer of boards, the wigwam is too tiny, and the single steering oar is used as a rudder rather than a sweep.

Figure 2.21. Cover of the 2014 Brendon Junior Classics for Young Readers edition. The artist is not identified. The board deck appears to be fastened by ropes to a log underpinning. Huck's steering oar—if that is what it is—looks more like a pole and is in any case not part of a pair of steering oars. The wigwam is no more than a piece of sagging canvas held up by corner posts. It is not raised and is not made of boards.

CHAPTER THREE

"Riding high like a duck"

Canoes, Boats, Ferries

Huck mentions many kinds of rivercraft on his journey south from St. Petersburg toward St. Louis, Cairo, and New Orleans: skiffs, canoes, drift canoes, steamboats, scows, trading scows, wood-flats, woodboats, keelboats, ferries, double-hull ferries, horse ferries, yawls, and wharfboats. How many readers today can describe any of these rivercraft? How many will know whether Huck's drift canoe was a dugout canoe or a birchbark canoe? How many can say what fuel was used to heat the water that made the steam that powered a steamboat, or explain where the steamboat captains acquired that fuel? How many can define the nautical terms *chute, crossing, warping,* and *quartering*? Some of the answers can be found by a close reading of *Huckleberry Finn,* but others require some historical research.

Early in *Huckleberry Finn* Huck's pap takes his son across the Mississippi River to a log shanty north of St. Petersburg:

> He said he would show who was Huck Finn's boss. So he watched out for me one day in the spring, and catched me, and took me up the river about three mile in a **skiff** and crossed over to the Illinois shore where it was woody and there warn't no houses but an old log hut in a place where the timber was so thick you couldn't find it if you didn't know where it was. (*HF* 29)

This is the first of several references to skiffs in the novel. Another skiff is the one that the thieves on the *Walter Scott* had planned to use as their means of escaping the doomed wreck. Huck and Jim find it—"there was the **skiff**, sure enough" (*HF* 86)—and take it. They row it back to the raft and unload it. Huck

uses that skiff to try to get help for the stranded thieves, then rows it back to
the raft "and sunk the **skiff**" (*HF* 92). Another skiff finds its way into the novel
when Huck leaves the raft and paddles his canoe out to try to find out how far
ahead Cairo is: "Right then, along comes a **skiff** with two men in it, with guns"
(*HF* 125; fig. 3.1). Still another skiff comes into play near the end of the novel
when the king and the duke escape their captors in the cemetery by stealing a
skiff to row to the raft: they were "just a laying to their oars and making their
skiff hum!" (*HF* 260).

What was a skiff?

A skiff was a small boat, similar to what we now call a rowboat, capable of
holding two or three people. A skiff was usually gracefully oval in shape, pointed at one end, and made of horizontal planks fastened to ribs. Although a skiff
might support a light sail, it was typically powered by a pair of oars that pivoted

Figure 3.1. E. W. Kemble's drawing of a skiff and a canoe (*HF* 126). The skiff with the
two slave hunters is reasonably accurate in the sense that it has a pointed front end and is
propelled by a set of oars in oarlocks. The oarsman has one hand on each oar. Huck holds
his single canoe paddle with both hands. Huck's canoe, however, is probably not accurately
drawn. It appears to be a dugout canoe rather than a birchbark canoe.

in oarlocks positioned opposite each other on the gunwales—that is, the upper rims of the boat. The rower had his hands on the inboard or dry ends of the oars. Usually the oarsman sat with his back to his destination. Sometimes, however, a skiff was rowed by a standing oarsman facing forward. Huck mentions a skiff being used to bring in a canoe:

> Well all at once, here comes a **canoe**; just a beauty, too, about thirteen or fourteen foot long, riding high like a duck. I shot head first off of the bank, like a frog, clothes and all on, and struck out for the **canoe**. I just expected there'd be somebody laying down in it, because people often done that to fool folks, and when a chap had pulled a **skiff** out most to it they'd raise up and laugh at him. But it warn't so this time. It was a **drift-canoe** sure enough, and I clumb in and **paddled** her ashore. (HF 37–38)

What was a canoe and what kind of a canoe does Huck find?

A canoe was narrower than a skiff and pointed at both ends. It was powered by a single paddle held with both hands. There were basically two kinds of canoes on the Mississippi River in Huck's time, and neither was made of planks. A dugout canoe was made of a single log hollowed out with small fires and woodcutting tools like axes, adzes, and chisels. A birchbark canoe was much lighter; it was made by fastening pieces of bark over a slender wooden frame and dabbing the joints with tar.

George Merrick, an early Mississippi steamboat pilot, described his own experiences with dugouts, "canoes hollowed out of white pine tree trunks. Some were large and long, and would carry four or five grown persons. Those owned and used by the boys were from six to eight feet long." Merrick described the dugouts that he and his brother used: "We each had a little pine '**dug-out**,' just large enough to carry one boy sitting in the stern, and a reasonable cargo of ducks, fish, or fruit. With such a load the gunwales of the craft were possibly three or four inches above the water line." Merrick also described birchbark canoes: "Of all the craft that ever floated, the birch-bark comes nearer being the ideal boat than any other. So light is it, that it may be carried on the head and shoulders for miles without great fatigue; and it sits on the water like a whiff of foam—a veritable fairy craft."[1]

Dugout canoes were heavy and clumsy to paddle and would have sat low in the water. Because a dugout, even empty, would scarcely have ridden "high like a duck," Huck's canoe is almost certainly a birchbark canoe. When Huck calls it a *drift canoe*, he means that it has drifted off from its owner and thus is free for the taking. It has not been stolen from its owner but was left unsecured on low ground and floated away when the river rose. A dugout canoe would not have been easily dislodged from its resting point on a riverbank. A birchbark canoe, because of its lightness, would have been quick to float away.

E. W. Kemble's several illustrations of Huck's canoe for the first US edition of *Huckleberry Finn* suggest that he thought it was a dugout canoe. As he has drawn the canoe, the side walls are thinner than on most dugouts; it rides higher on the water than a dugout would have ridden, and it has so little width that it would have been dangerously tippy without a stabilizing outrigger. One scholar has suggested that Kemble purposefully "rounded the canoe's stern and fit Huck so snugly into it that the shape cannot help suggesting a coffin" (fig. 3.2).[2] I think it is more likely that Kemble knew no more about canoes than he knew about lumber rafts. Kemble's drawing of Huck in his canoe on the night of the fog (fig. 3.3) suggests that he was not aware that a dugout canoe would have been particularly dangerous in rough weather or strong currents.

How do canoes function in the plot of *Huckleberry Finn*?

Huck's canoes could have been vitally important to the plot of *Huckleberry Finn*, but in fact they raise several unanswered questions about what role they actually do play. When Huck and Jim first escape on the raft from the men seeking Jim on Jackson's Island, they have a plan to use the canoe if they are caught: "If a boat was to come along we was going to take to the **canoe** and break for the Illinois shore" (*HF* 77). No boat comes along, so the canoe is not pressed into that kind of service.

A couple of weeks later, when they learn that they have drifted past Cairo in the fog, Huck and Jim, knowing that they cannot take the raft back up the Mississippi River to Cairo and then up the Ohio River to the free states, plan to use the canoe for their journey to freedom: "We talked it all over. It wouldn't do to take to the shore; we couldn't take the raft up stream, of course. There warn't no way but to wait for dark and start back in the **canoe** and take the chances" (*HF* 129).

Huck and Jim no sooner make that plan than the canoe disappears: "So we slept all day amongst the cottonwood thicket, so as to be fresh for the work, and when we went back to the raft about dark the **canoe** was gone!" (*HF* 129).

Figure 3.2. Another Kemble drawing of Huck's canoe (*HF* 43). The sides are too thin for a dugout canoe, and the canoe is too narrow to be stable. Huck's canoe was probably a birchbark canoe. One commentator has suggested that Kemble wanted to make it look as if Huck were in a coffin.

Huck does not explain why he and Jim decided not to sleep in their comfortably snug wigwam on the raft and thus guard the canoe that would take them to freedom. He does not explain why just this once they abandoned the raft that contains all that they own and instead slept in a cottonwood thicket. And he does not explain what happened to the canoe. Did it just drift away because they forgot to tie it up? Was it stolen? If it was stolen, why did the thief or thieves steal nothing else? Why does Huck never even think about, let alone try to solve, the mystery of the "gone" canoe?

Without the canoe Huck and Jim need a new plan. The obvious one would be to revive or revise the old plan to "sell the raft and get on a steamboat and go way up the Ohio amongst the free States and then be out of trouble" (*HF* 99). Their section of a lumber raft with around 384 cubic feet (4,600 board feet) of sawed lumber would have been worth a good bit of money, and there were

Figure 3.3. Kemble's drawing of Huck's canoe on the night of the fog (*HF* 101). A dugout canoe so long and narrow would have been dangerously tippy without an outrigger, especially when being maneuvered at night in rough currents and among snags.

plenty of steamboats heading up the Ohio to points north and east. Instead, Huck and Jim make a new plan, again involving a canoe:

> By and by we talked about what we better do, and found there warn't no way but just to go along down with the raft till we got a chance to buy a **canoe** to go back in. We warn't going to borrow it when there warn't anybody around, the way pap would do, for that might set people after us.
> So we shoved out, after dark, on the raft. (*HF* 129–30)

Huck never explains how they hope to have a chance to purchase a canoe, given that they are traveling only at night and hiding all day so no one will see them.

Several days after Huck and Jim are reunited on the raft at the end of the Grangerford-Shepherdson episode, Huck "finds" another canoe: "One morning about daybreak, I found a **canoe** and crossed over a **chute** to the main shore— it was only two hundred yards—and paddled about a mile up a crick amongst the cypress woods, to see if I couldn't get some berries" (*HF* 158). Huck gives no explanation of how he happens to have "found" this canoe. Twain originally wrote, "One morning about day-break, I **took the canoe** and crossed over a **chute**," apparently having forgotten that the canoe was "gone." He corrected the oversight by changing "**took the canoe**" to "**found a canoe**." The change is discussed in Fischer and Salamo's explanatory notes (*HF* 426–27). A *chute* was a narrow channel between an island and the riverbank. The main channel would have been on the other side of the island.

Huck also does not say how just taking the canoe is different from his pap's "borrowing" it, or why he no longer worries that a missing canoe will "set people after us." More important, having "found" the very canoe he had hoped to buy so that he and Jim can paddle it north to freedom, why can he think of nothing better to do with it now than paddle it up a creek and pick berries? The only "berries" Huck finds in his newfound canoe are a king and a duke. So much for the canoe as a means of escape from oppression.

In making his escape from his captor at the cemetery in which Peter Wilks has been buried, Huck finds one more unaccountably loose canoe: "I begun to look sharp for a boat to borrow; and the first time the lightning showed me one that wasn't chained, I snatched it and shoved. It was a **canoe**, and warn't fastened with nothing but a rope" (*HF* 258). When he is done with that one, he "filled up the **canoe** with water, and loaded rocks into her and sunk her where I could find her again when I wanted her" (*HF* 271). That is the canoe that the doctor uses to visit the raft to treat Tom Sawyer's wound. Canoes seem to come and go at the author's convenience in *Huckleberry Finn*. They apparently made so little impression on readers that virtually no cover illustrators have drawn a canoe, even though when Huck is on the raft a canoe is almost always tethered to it.

Huck makes several references to the steamboats he sees on his journey. One is the *Walter Scott*, wrecked in the middle of the Mississippi in chapters 12–13. The most important steamboat is the one that smashes into Huck and Jim's raft at the end of chapter 16:

It got to be very late and still, and then along comes a **steamboat** up the river. We lit the lantern, and judged she would see it. Up-stream boats didn't generly come close to us; they go out and follow the bars and hunt for easy water under the reefs; but nights like this they bull right up the channel against the whole river. (*HF* 130)

What was a steamboat?

A steamboat was a large passenger- and freight-carrying boat powered by a steam engine. It was typically propelled forward either by two matching side paddle wheels near the center of the boat or, later, by a single stern paddle wheel. Because a steamboat was powered by large steam-driven pistons pounding back and forth in big cylinders, it was notoriously noisy:

> We could hear her pounding along, but we didn't see her good till she was close. She aimed right for us. Often they do that and try to see how close they can come without touching; sometimes the wheel bites off a sweep. . . . All of a sudden she bulged out, big and scary, with a long row of wide-open **furnace-doors shining like red-hot teeth**, and her monstrous **bows** and **guards** hanging right over us. There was a yell at us, and a jingling of bells to stop the engines. (*HF* 130)

Huck clearly knows the basics of steamboat construction. The *bows* are the starboard (right) and larboard (left) foreparts of the steamboat. The *guards* are the safety guardrails. He also knows about the basic mechanics of steam engines. He later tells Tom Sawyer's Aunt Sally a lie: that his steamboat was delayed because "we blowed out a cylinder-head" (*HF* 279).

What fuel was used in the furnace boilers to make the steam?

Although coal was eventually used as steamboat fuel, in Huck's time the Mississippi steamboats were fueled almost exclusively by wood. What Huck and Jim see just before the steamboat crashes into their little raft is the orange glow of wood fires. To return to the brief passage from *Huckleberry Finn* that I quoted in chapter 1:

> I noticed some pieces of limbs and such things floating down, and a sprinkling of bark; so I knowed the river had begun to rise. I reckoned I would have great times, now, if I was over at the town. The June rise used to be always luck for me; because as soon as that rise begins, here comes **cord-wood** floating down, and pieces of log rafts—sometimes a dozen logs together; so all you have to do is to catch them and sell them to the **wood yards** and the sawmill. (*HF* 37)

What was cordwood?

Cordwood was wood split and cut into lengths so that it could be stacked ready for sale as firewood, the primary fuel for early steamboats. A cord was a stack of cut firewood 8 feet long, 4 feet wide, and 4 feet high, or a total of 128 cubic feet. In the context of *Huckleberry Finn*, cordwood was wood stacked ready to be sold to steamboats as fuel for their voracious boilers.

The early steamboats were fueled exclusively by wood—a *lot* of it. One early British traveler described his experience on the steamboat *Constitution* on a journey from New Orleans to Louisville, Kentucky, in the early 1830s: "The *Constitution* uses about twenty-six cords of wood per day; a cord consisting of about 128 cubic feet."[3] Twenty-six cords is enough firewood to fill an average modern two-car garage from front to back, side to side, and floor to ceiling.

Another early British traveler in the United States described the cotton-carrying steamboat he traveled on in 1846 on the Alabama River. He himself had a comfortable first-class cabin on the upper level, but others were not so fortunate: "The second class, or deck passengers, sleep where they can on the lower floor, where, besides the engine and the cotton, there are prodigious heaps of wood, which are devoured with marvelous rapidity by the furnace, and are as often restored at the different landings."[4] The steamboats did indeed have to stop often to load up on wood: "Steamboats rarely carried fuel supplies for more than twenty-four hours, and the common practice was to take on wood twice daily."[5]

Another early steamboat traveler on the Mississippi wrote about the amount of work done by slave deckhands in carrying firewood:

> The negroes of the Mississippi are happy specimens of God's image done up in ebony, and in many lighter colors, and they have frequently a deserved reputation as "deck-hands." It is astonishing what an amount of hard work they will perform, and yet retain their vivacity and spirits.... But the glory of the darkie deck-hand is in "wooding up." On a first-class steamer there may be sixty hands engaged in this exciting physical contest. The passengers extend themselves along the guards as spectators, and present a brilliant array. The performance consists in piling on the boat one hundred cords of wood in the shortest possible time.... The laborers pursue their calling with the precision of clock-work. Upon the shoulders of each is piled up innumerable sticks of wood, which are thus carried from the land into the capacious bowels of the steamer.[6]

The cordwood that Huck speaks of retrieving from the Mississippi and selling to a wood yard had apparently been stacked upstream close to the riverbank so that it could be sold to a passing steamboat. Before it could be sold, however, it had been carried off by the rising waters.

Cordwood was a valuable commodity in a river town, where it could easily be sold, resold, or bartered. Huck later refers to cordwood as a bartering substitute for cash. He reports that the duke sold fraudulent subscriptions to the local Pokeville newspaper:

> The price of the paper was two dollars a year, but he took in three subscriptions for half a dollar apiece on condition of them paying him in advance; they were going to pay in **cord-wood** and onions, as usual, but he said he had just bought the concern and knocked down the price as low as he could afford it, and was going to run it for cash. (*HF* 174)

Near the start of chapter 19, having tied up and concealed the raft, Huck is watching the day come up. On the other side of the river he sees a log cabin and a stack of cordwood:

> You see the mist curl up off the water, and the east reddens up, and the river, and you make out a log cabin on the edge of the woods, away on the bank on t'other side of the river, being a **wood-yard**, likely, and piled by them cheats so you can throw a dog through it anywhere. (*HF* 157)

Huck is here referring to the practice of some dishonest wood sellers (the "cheats") of stacking the wood so loosely that the spaces or gaps in the cords are big enough to throw a dog through. When he first wrote that passage, however, Twain made no mention of the wood yard: "You would see the lightest and whitest mist curling up from the water; pretty soon the east reddens up, then the river reddens, and maybe you make out a little log cabin on the edge of the forest, away yonder on the bank on t'other side of the river" (*HF* 474). The bit about the wood yard and the swindling "cheats" was added in revision, along with several other changes that made the passage less lyrical and more cynical.

What was a wood yard?

In the context of *Huckleberry Finn*, a wood yard is a commercial enterprise adjacent to a navigable river that sells seasoned firewood to passing steamboats. In the really early days of steamboat travel, steamboats had to stop and send their own work crews out to cut firewood from the forests on the riverbanks. That made for slow progress, especially for steamboats going upstream, because the boilers had to operate at full capacity to fight the current. As the forests were culled from the banks of the rivers and as farmers settled on the land back from the riverbanks, the steamboat engineers began to negotiate with the farmers to buy cordwood. The farmers were delighted to discover that they had a ready and steady cash crop at their fingertips cutting, splitting, and stacking firewood for the steamboats. The steamboat captains, for their part, were delighted to buy the cut and seasoned cordwood from these local farmers. Before long, commercial wood yards opened, each with its own landing where steamboats could tie up while their deckhands worked alongside the wood-yard crews to carry the wood onto their lower decks and stack it there (fig. 3.4).

Figure 3.4. Carrying cordwood onto a steamboat. This drawing by Jacob A. Dallas was published with the article "Up the Mississippi," in the October 1857 issue of *Emerson's Magazine and Putnam's Monthly*, on page 453. Dallas was a mid-nineteenth-century American artist who had lived in Missouri as a youth, then moved to the East Coast. In the early 1850s he visited New Orleans and traveled on the Mississippi River in preparation for a series of renderings of scenes of river life. In this drawing he shows the first-class passengers partying on the upper deck of the steamboat while the laborers and deck passengers do the actual work of loading the firewood.

Typical of these wood yards is the one mentioned by the early traveler James
Stuart:

> In the course of the 10th of April [1830], while we were still in the territory of
> the Arkansas, and in a very wild part of the river, we stopped to take in wood [at]
> the residence of a planter, who was a judge, by which I mean a justice of [the]
> peace, in the neighborhood. The judge was a fine old man, in very comfortable
> habitation, clean and well kept. . . . His plantation is on the edge of the river, and
> he has rather a nice orchard and garden, and large stacks of wood ready for the
> steamboats.[7]

Supplying wood for steamboats, then, was clearly a profitable business. The
local wood-yard operator in St. Petersburg would have been eager to buy any
cordwood that Huck brought in because he would have had a ready and steady
outlet for it (fig. 3.5).

Huck mentions several other wood yards. In chapter 16 the slave hunter
Parker directs Huck away from a town to avoid infecting it with smallpox by
saying "it's only a **wood yard**" (*HF* 127). Huck mentions another wood yard at
the shared "steamboat landing" (*HF* 144) that is the site of the Grangerford-
Shepherdson shoot-out in chapter 18. The store owner is obviously in the business of selling cordwood to passing steamboats. Huck is hiding in a tree above
the wood yard watching the feuding families kill each other:

> There was a **wood-rank**, four foot high, a little ways in front of the tree, and at
> first I was going to hide behind that; but maybe it was luckier I didn't.
>
> There was four or five men cavorting around on their horses in the open place
> before the log store, cussing and yelling, and trying to get at a couple of young
> chaps that was behind the **wood-rank** alongside of the steamboat landing—but
> they couldn't come it [*sic*]. Every time one of them showed himself on the river
> side of the **wood pile** he got shot at. The two boys was squatting back to back
> behind the **pile**, so they could watch both ways.
>
> By and by the men stopped cavorting around, and yelling. They started riding
> towards the store; then up gets one of the boys, draws a steady bead over the
> **wood-rank**, and drops one of them out of his saddle. All the men jumped off of
> their horses and grabbed the hurt one and started to carry him to the store; and
> that minute the two boys started on the run. They got half way to the tree I was
> in, before the men noticed. Then the men see them, and jumped on their horses

and took out after them. They gained on the boys, but it didn't do no good, the boys had too good a start; they got to the **wood pile** that was in front of my tree, and slipped behind it, and so they had the bulge on the men again. (*HF* 152–53).

What was a wood rank?

According to Mississippi pilot George Merrick, a wood rank was a long, high woodpile. Merrick's vivid account testifies to the fact that some operators of wood yards were "pirates" or what Huck called "cheats":

> As second clerk, I was early taught to hold my own with the pirates who conducted the woodyards scattered along the river, from which the greater part of the fuel used on old-time river boats was purchased. There was a great variety of

Figure 3.5. A wood yard on the Mississippi. This was also drawn by Jacob Dallas for the article "Up the Mississippi" and appeared on page 452. The chubby man with the pipe runs the wood yard and anticipates selling cordwood to the approaching steamboat. He can offer two options: the wood rank (woodpile) on the bank to his left or the loaded wood-flat (boat) in front of him in the water. If the steamboat officers choose the latter, they will tie the wood-flat alongside and unload it as they proceed upriver. When it is empty, they will cast it loose to drift back with the current to the wood yard. Note the steering oar (or sweep) attached to the wood-flat. There would have been a matching oar at the other end. These sweeps would be used to guide the empty wood-flat sideways as the current carried it back to the wood yard.

wood offered for sale, and a greater diversity in the manner of piling it. . . . For convenience, the woodmen usually put twenty cords in a **rank**. . . . Woodmen who cared for their reputation and avoided a "scrap" with the clerks, captains, and mates of steamboats usually made their **twenty-cord ranks** eighty-four feet long and eight feet high. Such dealers also piled their sticks parallel to each other in the **ranks**; they also threw out the rotten and very crooked ones. . . .

It took the "pirates" to start the music, however. When only [a] scant eighty feet were found in the **rank**, with rotten and green wood sandwiched in all through the tiers, and crooked limbs and crossed sticks in all directions, it became the duty of the clerk to estimate his discount. After running his rod over it, he would announce, before the first stick was taken off by the deck hands, the amount of wood in the **rank**. . . . When the mate could stand behind the **rank** and see, through a cross-piled hole, more than half the length of the steamboat, it was deemed a rather acute case, calling for an eighteen-cord decision.[8]

The ranks in *Huckleberry Finn* are only four feet high, not eight, so we can probably assume either that they are twice as long to make them twenty-cord ranks or that they are considered half-ranks of ten cords each. It may be, however, that Huck does not mean to be so precise in his use of the noun *rank*. He may simply mean a large stack of cordwood ready to be loaded onto a steamboat.

In a comic scene near the end of chapter 7 of *Huckleberry Finn*, Jim tells Huck about his past business investments. He once had fourteen dollars, he says. He lost nine dollars on a cow that died and invested the remaining five dollars in the "bank" of a one-legged slave who promised to pay him thirty-five dollars at the end of the year:

> "So I done it. Den I reck'n'd I'd inves' de thirty-five dollars right off en keep things a-movin'. Dey wuz a nigger name' Bob, dat had ketched a **wood-flat**, en his marster didn' know it; en I bought it off'n him en told him to take de thirty-five dollars when de en' er de year come; but somebody stole de **wood-flat** dat night, en nex' day de one-laigged nigger say de bank's busted. So dey didn' none uv us git no money." (*HF* 56)

What was a wood-flat?

Most editors of *Huckleberry Finn* are silent about what a wood-flat was. Some make wild guesses, like the person who wrote the SparkNotes online "translation" of *Huckleberry Finn* (cited in chapter 1) into "modern English." He or she translates *wood-flat* as "wooden flat" and annotates *flat* as "a piece of straight timber used to build ships." A wood-flat was nothing of the sort. I have found only three editors who make a serious effort to define it, and they get it only partly right. One tells us that a wood-flat was "a flat-bottomed boat for transporting lumber," another that it was "a raft or flat-bottomed boat used for carrying timber," and still another that it was a "raft or barge for transporting wood."[9]

Wood-flats were indeed flat-bottomed boats, but they were not rafts and were not used for transporting either timber (i.e., logs) or lumber (i.e., wood sawed lengthwise for building houses, barns, boats, and furniture). In the context of *Huckleberry Finn*, a wood-flat is a large flat-bottomed bargelike boat that was used to hold firewood until it was sold to a passing upstream steamboat. Sometimes a northbound captain would buy a wood-flat full of firewood, tie it to the side of his steamboat, and then proceed up the river while the wood-yard employees, the steamship crew, and perhaps the deck passengers unloaded the cordwood and stacked it on the deck. When the wood-flat was empty, the wood-yard laborers would cut it loose to drift back to the wood yard so it could be refilled for the next northbound steamboat. Downstream boats had to tie up and load the cordwood while stationary before casting off to continue their journey south. They would not tow a wood-flat south because cutting it loose when empty would let the river currents take the empty boat farther south, away from the wood yard it belonged to. Historian Louis Hunter described the practice of upstream steamboats towing flatboats:

> In order to reduce the time lost in "wooding" the larger and faster boats came to adopt the practice on upstream trips of taking **flatboats** of **cordwood** in tow. With but a slight interruption of its journey while the **wood boats** were made fast, the steamboat took on its fuel supply while proceeding up the river, and the **wood boats** when empty were cast loose to drift back to the **woodyard**.[10]

Conor Carey, the curator at the Arabia Steamboat Museum in Kansas City, told me that in 1853 a slave had been engaged to help unload firewood from two towed wood-flats onto the deck of the steamboat *Arabia*. While doing so, the slave slipped, fell overboard, and drowned. The owner of the slave then sued the steamboat company for reimbursement for the value of the slave. As a result of the lawsuit a deckhand gave a deposition that stated, "We got a flat-boat of wood in tow, each side" (personal correspondence).

A generic term for the class of boat we are speaking of is *flatboat*. A drawing in a book dated 1891 (fig. 3.6) depicts a large rectangular boat with vertical sides and slanted ends. Labeled "A Mississippi Flat-Boat," it shows a bargelike boat meant to float with the current. The two men with steering oars could have moved it short distances in or out of the main channel. The drawing shows one oarsman on the end and one on the side, although such boats were typically steered with the sweeps at opposite ends. This flatboat is loaded with boxes and barrels of trade goods. It is not roofed over, but there is a large wigwamlike structure in the very center, apparently used as sleeping quarters for the crew of four and a dog.

How big were these flatboats?

The short answer is pretty darn big. A fair approximation can be derived from a comment that Twain made in *Life on the Mississippi*, where he talked brief-ly about the early commerce on the river, especially the commerce involving

Figure 3.6. A drawing of a flatboat on the Mississippi River, reproduced from Samuel Adams Drake's *The Making of the Great West, 1512–1883* (1891). The large wigwam in the center might have slept the four crewmen. The sweeps are oddly positioned. Normally they would have been located at opposite ends of the vessel, where they could move the current-driven flatboat short distances from side to side.

keelboats and broadhorns: "The river's earliest commerce was in **great barges—keelboats, broadhorns**. They floated and sailed from the upper rivers to New Orleans, changed cargoes there, and were tediously warped and poled back by hand" (*LM* 238). We will define *keelboat* and *warp* later in this chapter, but first I want to consider the term *broadhorn*.

Twain never used the term *broadhorn* in *Huckleberry Finn*, but it was another name for what he called a flatboat. I quote from an anonymous article published in 1858:

> One of the peculiar features in the system of rivers which forms the Mississippi is the **flat-boat** (built of gunwales and plank), some **one hundred feet long and thirty broad**, square at the ends—familiarly known as "**broad-horns**." Some are roofed over, others are open, and they carry the loads of **giants**. On every tributary these arks are constructed through the summer and fall, ready to do their work when the hour shall come. And when that time does come, and the myriads of corn-fields, large and small, pour their crops together, these "**broad-horns**" receive them into their **capacious** chambers, and are swept downward by the stream.[11]

A flatboat used to store cordwood for sale to steamboats had the more specific name wood-flat. Because the steamboats needed so much cordwood, the wood-flats had to be large. The *Constitution*, we recall, needed twenty-six cords a day. Twain hinted at the size of a wood-flat in chapter 11 of *Life on the Mississippi*, where he wrote of seeing families forced out of their riverside homes by floods living on their wood-flats: "The family and the few farm-animals were huddled together in an empty **wood-flat** riding at her moorings close at hand. In this **flatboat** the family would have to cook and eat and sleep for a lesser or greater number of days (or possibly weeks), until the river should fall two or three feet and let them get back to their log-cabin" (*LM* 293). Note that Twain used the terms *wood-flat* and *flatboat* almost, but not quite, as synonyms. When such a vessel was loaded with cordwood for sale to upstream steamboats, it was a wood-flat, but when it was used as a temporary haven for people and animals, it was a flatboat or, more precisely, an "empty wood-flat." The boat itself was the same; only its name changed with its contents and particular function.

In chapter 13 of *Huckleberry Finn*, Huck uses the term *woodboat* in connection with his attempt to send help to the thieves trapped on the wreck of the

Walter Scott: "I went back and got into my skiff and bailed her out and then pulled up shore in the easy water about six hundred yards, and tucked myself in among some **woodboats**" (*HF* 91). Huck apparently here uses the term *wood-boat* as a synonym for *wood-flat*.

Huck also sometimes uses the term *scow* as a synonym for *flatboat*. When he is discovered hiding among the bundles of shingles on the huge lumber raft in chapter 16, Huck at first gives his name as Charles William Allbright, the name of the dead baby in the barrel story. The raftsman Davy asks him what his real name is. This time he gives his name as Aleck James Hopkins, and the conversation continues:

> "Well, Aleck, where did you come from, here?"
>
> "From a **trading scow**. She lays up the bend yonder. I was born on her. Pap has traded up and down here all his life; and he told me to swim off here, because when you went by he said he would like to get some of you to speak to a Mr. Jonas Turner, in Cairo, and tell him—"
>
> "O, come!" . . .
>
> "Now looky-here," says Davy; "you're scared, and so you talk wild. Honest, now, do you live in a scow, or is it a lie?"
>
> "Yes, sir, in a **trading scow**. She lays up at the head of the bend. But I warn't born in her. It's our first trip." (*HF* 122)

We can tell from the context that the trading scow Huck imagines is a boat large enough for a family to live in and conduct a trading business of some sort. This particular scow would probably be at least partly roofed over to keep the family and the trade goods dry. But not all scows were used as houseboats. An early traveler on the Mississippi described scows in a way that makes them sound like flatboats that could be used as wood-flats:

> At the bank, near the wood-cutter's shanty, are tied two or more **broad scows**, in which the wood is piled in cords. . . . Boats coming down the river are obliged to round-to and tie up, while taking wood aboard; in going up stream, the steamer runs her nose between the two **scows**, and, with one in tow on either side, goes steaming up, all hands working sharp to get the wood aboard, when the **scows** are cast off, and, in charge of the owner, float down again to their station.[12]

To judge from that passage, a scow was a large flat-bottomed bargelike boat that could serve any of several purposes. Some scows might be converted to houseboats, but others served as wood-flats.

In chapter 20 of *Life on the Mississippi*, Twain gave further evidence of the size of wood-flats. In his account of the catastrophic explosion of the steamship *Pennsylvania*, Twain reported that the steamboat was going upstream "on a half-head of steam, towing a **wood-flat** which was fast being emptied" (*LM* 355). Then, suddenly, four of the eight boilers exploded, leaving many crew and passengers dead or wounded: "They drew the **wood-boat** aft, and they [the mates] and the captain fought back the frantic herd of frightened immigrants till the wounded could be brought there and placed in safety first. . . . The fire drove all into the **wood-flat** that could be accommodated there; it was cut adrift, then, and it and the burning steamer floated down the river toward Ship Island. They moored the flat at the head of the island" (*LM* 356–57). Twain did not report how many were on the wood-flat, but a survivor, W. G. Mepham, reported later that at least 180 passengers had been carried to safety on it.[13] For a wood-flat to carry so many people, it must have been sizable.

A wood-flat, then, might be defined as a large flat-bottomed boat, sometimes called either a scow or a broadhorn, that provided firewood for steamboats. Because it was designed to be attached to an upstream steamboat, towed along upstream while it was being unloaded, and then cut loose, we can easily understand why the slave Bob would have been able to "ketch" a loose one as it floated by, why it was worth so much to Jim, and why someone would have wanted to steal it from Jim.

One of the uses of a steamboat was to serve as a ferry that carried passengers and freight from one side of the river to the other. We see one in chapter 8 of *Huckleberry Finn*, the steam ferry that had set out from St. Petersburg to hunt for and try to retrieve Huck's supposedly murdered body. Another plays a role in chapter 13 when Huck, who has recently escaped from the wreck of the *Walter Scott*, makes a good-hearted effort to save the lives of the gang of thieves and murderers still trapped there:

We seen a light, now, away down to the right, on shore. So I said I would go for it. The skiff was half full of plunder which that gang had stole, there on the wreck. We hustled it onto the raft in a pile, and I told Jim to float along down, and show a light when he judged he had gone about two mile and keep it burning till I come;

then I manned my oars and shoved for the light. As I got down towards it, three or four more showed—up on a hillside. It was a village. I closed in above the shore-light, and laid on my oars and floated. As I went by, I see it was a lantern hanging on the jackstaff of a **double-hull ferry boat**. Everything was dead still, nobody stirring. I floated in under the stern, made fast, and clumb aboard. (*HF* 88)

What was a double-hull ferryboat?

The hull was the part of a vessel that went into the water. Most boats and ships had only a single hull. Single-hull rivercraft were easier to build than double-hull ones, but they tended to be more tippy and to ride deeper in the water. The double hull would have been particularly useful for a ferry because it would have given passengers a steadier ride and, with its shallower draft, would have been able to go closer to the shore to pick up and discharge passengers and freight (fig. 3.7). It would also have made possible a much larger deck space for the passengers and freight—and thus have been more profitable, especially at busy crossings like St. Louis.

Huck wakes up the drowsy ferryboat captain and tells him a pack of lies to get him to fire up his steamboat and go rescue the gang of thieves on the *Walter Scott*. One of the lies is about an imaginary Miss Hooker:

"She was a visiting, there at Booth's Landing, and just in the edge of the evening she started over with her nigger woman in the **horse-ferry**, to stay all night at her friend's house, Miss What-you-may-call-her, I disremember her name, and they lost their **steering-oar**, and swung around and went a-floating down, stern-first, about two mile, and **saddle-baggsed** on the wreck, and the ferry man and the nigger woman and the horses was all lost, but Miss Hooker she made a grab and got aboard the wreck." (*HF* 90)

For a rivercraft to "saddlebag" on a stationary boat, rock, or island was to hit it sideways in such force that it bent around the stationary object. The equestrian term comes from the saddlebag that was carried bent over a horse, one pouch on either side of the horse's back.

What was a horse ferry?

Almost no Twain scholar has attempted to explain what a horse ferry was. The only scholar to do so that I am aware of was Emory Elliott, who said that a

Figure 3.7. A steamboat landing on the lower Mississippi River. This is another of the river-scene drawings by Jacob Dallas for the magazine article "Up the Mississippi," appearing on page 435. Just in the center, perched on a slanting hillside, is a double-hull houseboat. Such a boat, the forerunner of the modern catamaran, would have been steadier than a single-hull boat and would have been able to operate in shallower water. A double-hull ferry would have had a somewhat similar construction. The decaying structure in the foreground, just to the right of the cows and pigs, is apparently the rotting remains of an old flatboat.

horse ferry was a "ferry designed to carry horses and wagons."[14] That is surely wrong, however. For one thing, it would be puzzling indeed to have a second steam ferry so close to the one owned and operated by the man Huck is addressing, especially since that man's business is none too prosperous: "I'm the captain, and the owner, and the mate, and the pilot, and watchman, and head deck-hand; and sometimes I'm the freight and passengers" (HF 88). It would also be strange to have a ferry designed to specialize in transporting horses and wagons. What would be the advantage in such a specialty? And if there were such a ferry, why would Miss Hooker be riding on it? She was neither a horse nor a wagon.

No, a horse ferry was not a ferry built to *transport* horses, it was a ferry *powered by* horses.[15] The first passenger-carrying horse ferry in the United States took its maiden trip in 1814 in New York City, between Manhattan and Brooklyn. Powered by horses walking around in a circle on the deck, it was faster and more reliable than the rowboats and sailing scows it soon put out of business.

The horse ferry was so successful that other designers soon built more efficient horse ferries. Instead of walking around a central post on the deck, the horses soon walked in place on a horizontal circular treadmill, and after that on roll-type treadmills similar to the treadmills now seen in exercise gyms around the world. Inventors also experimented with various means of propulsion for horse-powered boats: side paddle wheels, rear paddle wheels, and underwater screw-type propellers. Horse ferries, sometimes called teamboats or horse-boats, were not as fast, large, or powerful as the steamboats that were already in use for longer runs up and down America's rivers, but for shorter runs across rivers they were far cheaper to build and to operate. They were nimbler because they drew less water, and they were safer. They did not catch fire, and the horses never blew up. From that first crossing to Brooklyn in 1814, the horse-powered ferry quickly made its way westward (figs. 3.8 through 3.10).

Until 1820, the usual way to cross the Mississippi River into St. Louis was to be rowed across in a flat-bottomed scow, or "flat." That year two companies had efficient eight-horse ferries licensed to make the crossing. On April 19 the *St. Louis Enquirer* ran this notice:

> The public are [*sic*] congratulated on the establishment of the new ferry boats at St. Louis. Mr. [Samuel R.] Wiggins and Mr. [John] Dey have each started a boat propelled by eight horses, which make passages in a few minutes across this broad and rapid stream. The boats have cabins for the accommodation of the passengers, where they sit as comfortably as in the chamber of a hotel. Mr. Wiggins' boat is particularly elegant. By the establishment of these ferries the river is now crossed regularly and rapidly, with safety and convenience, and at a much cheaper rate than in common flats.[16]

Business was so brisk in St. Louis that Wiggins eventually replaced his horse-powered ferry with a steamboat ferry. A decade later the British traveler James Stuart, visiting St. Louis, noted, "There is a steam ferryboat across the river. . . . The first boat put upon the river was a teamboat; and it answered so well, that a steamboat has now been established."[17] By the term *teamboat*, of course, he meant a boat powered by a team of horses. Stuart found that there was still a horse ferry crossing the Missouri River a few miles north, at St. Charles:

> On reaching the shore of the river opposite to St. Charles, we observed the team ferryboat leaving the opposite bank, but the current was so rapid that she was

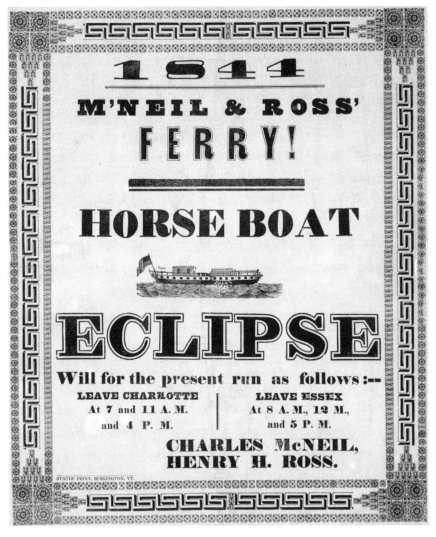

Figure 3.8. An 1844 broadside advertisement for a horse ferry. The *Eclipse* ran across the lower end of Lake Champlain between Charlotte, Vermont, and Essex, New York. (M'Neil & Ross Ferry, *Horse Boat Eclipse*, 1844; ink on paper, approximately 9 x 17 inches; Shelburne Museum, Vermont, gift of Mrs. Patrick Hill, 1981–59.2; photograph by Andy Duback)

Figure 3.9. A horse ferry at Cassville, Wisconsin. This photo was taken around 1900. The horses walked on a treadmill that powered the two side paddle wheels. (Courtesy of the State Historical Society of Wisconsin, image no. 90626)

Figure 3.10. A drawing of a boat powered by horses from the magazine *American Mercury*, September 24, 1842.

three-quarters of an hour in crossing to the south bank, though the distance is not much more than half a mile. We succeeded, by running some way along the shore, in recrossing in the teamboat in ten minutes.[18]

As for the lost steering oar that Huck mentions, the early horse ferries did not have built-in rudders, so they were guided by a removable oar similar to a sweep but used as a rudder. Because the horse ferry had its own source of power—the horses—only the one oar was necessary to guide it. A reconstructed

1885 horse-powered boat, with the steering oar clearly visible, appears on page 143 in Kevin Crisman and Arthur Cohn's 1998 book, *When Horses Walked on Water*. According to Huck's fabricated story about the horse ferry at Booth's Landing, the steersman had somehow lost the steering oar, thus leaving the ferry adrift in the current. Huck did not say what caused the steersman to lose the oar.

In the lead-up to the Wilks episode mentioned earlier, the king offers a canoe ride to a man who is heading to the ferryboat landing. The king pumps the man for information about the life, death, friends, family, and fortunes of the recently deceased Peter Wilks. He decides that he and the duke will impersonate the British brothers of the dead man. To do that he realizes that they need to come into town not on a raft, a canoe, or even a small steamboat but in style on a big steamboat from Cincinnati:

> She sent out her **yawl**, and we went aboard, and she was from Cincinnati; and when they found we only wanted to go four or five mile, they was booming mad, and give us a cussing, and said they wouldn't land us. But the king was ca'm. He says:
> "If gentlemen kin afford to pay a dollar a mile, apiece, to be took on and put off in a **yawl**, a steamboat kin afford to carry 'em, can't it?"
> So they softened down and said it was all right; and when we got to the village, they **yawled** us ashore. (*HF* 208–9)

What was a yawl?

A yawl was a four-oar skiff, or rowboat, normally tethered to a larger boat and used to transport passengers and freight to and from the shore. A yawl was particularly necessary for big steamboats, which drew too much water to go in close to the shore where the river was shallow. A yawl was usually associated with larger steamboats, but smaller steam ferries sometimes had smaller skiffs that could be used to take passengers to or from otherwise inaccessible locations. In chapter 15 of *Tom Sawyer*, Tom sneaks a free ride in the skiff that is tethered to the St. Petersburg ferry: "He crept down the bank, watching with all his eyes, slipped into the water, swam three or four strokes, and climbed into the skiff that did '**yawl**' duty at the boat's stern. He laid himself down under the **thwarts** and waited, panting" (*TS* 99). A thwart is a crosspiece holding the gunwales apart and often serving as a seat for a rower.

When Huck gets to the Phelps place in chapter 32 of *Huckleberry Finn*, he tells Sally Phelps, who thinks he is Tom Sawyer, a hastily made-up lie about having just gotten off a steamboat:

> "The boat landed just at daylight, and I left my baggage on the **wharfboat** and went looking around town and out a piece in the country, to put in time and not get here too soon; and so I come down the back way."
>
> "Who'd you give the baggage to?"
>
> "Nobody."
>
> "Why, child, it'll be stole!"
>
> "Not where I hid it I reckon it won't," I says. (*HF* 279)

What was a wharfboat?

A wharfboat was a large boat tethered to the bank of the river (fig. 3.11). It was designed to serve as a kind of floating dock that would rise and fall with the rising and falling river levels.

The following 1857 description showed that a wharfboat was a place where steamboats could tie up to load and unload people and cargo, thus saving them the trouble, time, and expense of using a yawl. It also shows why Tom Sawyer's Aunt Sally is concerned about the security of the baggage Huck says he had left there:

> The rise and fall of the river being so great, permanent wharves are impossible; their place is supplied, at all stopping places of any business, with a floating dock, called a **wharf-boat**. This, being tied to the bank, rises and falls with the floods, and is thus safe and convenient. It is the centre of activity, and usually is thronged upon the arrival or departure of boats. In it, too, all perishable goods may be stored, for which you may expect round charges to be made, particularly if you are not a resident of the place; for it is the rule, the civilized world through, to fleece travelers—they are secure only in some few barbarous countries.
>
> About these **wharf-boats** congregate all the idle and good-for-nothing fellows of the town, who, having no steady occupation, hope to pick up some job which will keep them supplied with the two things needful—whisky and tobacco.[19]

During his visit to the huge lumber raft in what is often referred to as the raft episode in chapter 16 of *Huckleberry Finn*, from his hiding place among the piles of shingles Huck witnesses the raftsmen at their leisure having a good

Figure 3.11. A wharfboat ready for the approach of a steamboat. The wharfboat was tethered to the riverbank. As a floating pier or landing dock, it could be let out or brought back in as the river fell or rose. It was on a such a wharfboat that Huck says he has left his baggage. The drawing is by Jacob Dallas for the article "Up the Mississippi," on page 453.

time singing, bragging, and fighting. That ends when the men are called to their posts for a crossing: "Just then there was a loud order to stand by for a **crossing**, and some of them went forward to man the sweeps there, and the rest went aft to handle the after sweeps. I laid still and waited for fifteen minutes, and had a smoke out of a pipe that one of them left in reach; then the **crossing** was finished" (*HF* 111). What was a crossing? In the context of chapter 16, a crossing was an activity required of the crew of a large raft so that the raft could stay in the main channel even though the channel itself had shifted from one side of the river to the other. If the crew did not use the sweeps to keep the raft in the main channel, the raft would lose its downstream momentum and risk colliding with the riverbank or a northbound steamboat crossing in the other direction (*HF* 78).

When the crossing is completed, the raftsmen "stumped back and had a

drink around and went to talking and singing again. Next they got out an old
fiddle, and one played, and another patted Juba, and the rest turned themselves
loose on a regular old-fashioned **keel-boat** break-down" (*HF* 111–12).

To pat Juba was to clap hands or slap thighs. A "break-down" was a fast-
paced dance, of African origin, sometimes called a hoedown (fig. 3.12). But
what was a keelboat? Twain uses the term only this once in *Huckleberry Finn*.
By the 1840s, after all, keelboats had all but ceased to exist on the Mississippi
River.

Figure 3.12. A hoedown on a Mississippi flatboat. An early traveler on the Mississippi
River wrote of the hard work that slaves did in carrying wood into a steamboat and in
entertaining the white boatmen: "With professional flatboatmen they are always favorites,
and at night . . . the master of the [fiddle] will touch off the 'Arkansas traveler,' and then
gradually sliding into a 'Virginia hoe-down,' he will be accompanied by a genuine darkie
keeping time on the light fantastic heal-and-toe tap." T. B. Thorpe, "Remembrances of the
Mississippi," *Harper's New Monthly Magazine*, December, 1855, 37.

What was a keelboat?

A keelboat differed from a flatboat by having a curved bottom that sloped up on either side of a keel, a structural projection that divided the boat lengthwise and helped keep the vessel from drifting sideways in the water. On a riverboat the keel was not deep—often just a few inches—but it helped to keep the boat going in a straight line. In going downstream the keelboat drifted with the current, but it might be assisted by oars, poles, or a sail. With great effort it could be taken back upstream. T. B. Thorpe's illustrated (fig. 3.13) 1855 magazine article, which Twain might have consulted, described the keelboats and the men who in the early days struggled to take them back up the Mississippi:

> The **keel-boat** was long and narrow, sharp at the bow and stern, and of light draft. From fifteen to twenty "hands" were required to propel it along. The crew, divided equally on each side, took their places upon the "walking-boards" extending along the whole length of the craft, and, setting one end of their pole in the bottom of the river, the other was brought to the shoulder, and with body bent forward, they *walked* the boat against the formidable current.[20]

Keelboats were rarely in use at the time *Huckleberry Finn* is set. In the lead-in to chapter 3 of *Life on the Mississippi*, Twain said that the earliest commerce on the river "was in great barges—**keelboats**. . . . They floated and sailed from the upper rivers to New Orleans, changed cargoes there, and were tediously warped and poled back by hand" (*LM* 238). *Warp* in that context was a nautical term for hauling a vessel. To warp a boat upriver, a long rope was tied to a tree or a rock upstream, and then the crew on the vessel would haul on the rope.

When steamboats put keelboats out of business, the keelboatmen had to find other work. Some of them got work on a steamboat, but many found work "on a pine raft constructed in the forests up toward the sources of the Mississippi" (*LM* 239). To show readers of *Life on the Mississippi* what these ex-keelboatmen were like, Twain decided to "throw in" (*LM* 239) a chapter, now usually referred to as the raft episode, from his unfinished novel, *Adventures of Huckleberry Finn*. It is understandable, then, that the partying of the old-time keelboaters should still be in evidence on the huge lumber raft in chapter 16. Many of the raftsmen in the raft episode would once have worked on keelboats, after all, and their dancing would have been appropriately referred to as "a regular old-fashioned **keel-boat** break-down."

Figure 3.13. A keelboat being propelled upstream against the current. Unlike a flatboat, the keelboat had tapered ends and a rounded hull. The main part of the surface was roofed in. The keelboat floated down the Mississippi loaded with trade goods. Walkways on both sides of the boat gave the pole pushers a secure place from which to "walk" the keelboat back upriver close to the riverbank, where the river was usually shallow and the current slow. Keelboats like this were eventually put out of business by steamboats. Thorpe, "Remembrances," 29.

The raft episode, and the controversy about whether it should be published in the novel, is the subject of the next chapter. I close this chapter with a curious incident in the raft episode. Near the end of the episode the raftsman Ed tells the story of Dick Allbright and the haunted barrel. Part of the story runs thus:

> "Well, he [Dick Allbright] raised up two or three times, and looked away off and around on the water. That started me at it, too. A body is always doing what he sees somebody else doing, though there mayn't be no sense in it. Pretty soon I see a black something floating on the water away off to stabboard and **quartering** behind us. . . .
>
> "By and by I says, 'Why looky-here, Dick Allbright, that thing's a-gaining on us, I believe.' He never said nothing. The thing gained and gained. . . .
>
> "It floated right along abreast, now, and didn't gain any more. It was about twenty foot off." (*HF* 114–15)

What does Ed mean by *quartering*?

I have seen only one attempt to define that term as it is used in *Huckleberry Finn*: "**quarter**—To sustain a position behind a vessel. The view from any vessel is divided into four parts: the port bow and starboard bow forward, and the port quarter and starboard quarter astern" (*HF* 456). Surely, however, Fischer and Salamo are wrong to suggest that for the barrel to quarter behind the raft is to sustain or maintain a position there. Ed uses the term not when the barrel has locked into a spot twenty feet behind the right rear corner of the raft, but earlier, when it is so far away from the raft that he can scarcely see it.

A better sense of the meaning of quartering can be found at the start of chapter 15 in *The Adventures of Tom Sawyer* when Tom wades and swims from Jackson's Island over to the Illinois riverbank:

> A few minutes later Tom was in the shoal water of the bar, wading toward the Illinois shore. Before the depth reached his middle he was half-way over; the current would permit no more wading, now, so he struck out confidently to swim the remaining hundred yards. He swam **quartering** upstream, but still was swept downward rather faster than he had expected. (*TS* 99)

Tom knows that if he wants to swim to a spot directly across the river, he has to aim for a spot well above it, because the current will sweep him down toward his actual destination. Similarly, a person rowing a boat across a river had to head his boat at an angle upstream, knowing that the current would pull him downstream to his actual destination. To quarter, then, is to compensate for the speed of the current by moving not straight toward one's destination but above it.

A barrel is not a boat, but this floating barrel sometimes acts like one. Whoever or whatever was powering the haunted barrel, then, was aiming for a spot well ahead of the raft—that is, was quartering toward it—knowing that the current would sweep the barrel downward right to the raft. We cannot know for sure the source of that power, but it was presumably the only occupant of the barrel, the dead baby Charles William Allbright. If it was he, then young Charles was a fine navigator.

We might wish that Huck had explained some of his nautical terms more fully, but we can scarcely fault Twain for not anticipating that readers a century and more after he wrote his book would not be aware of the meanings of some of his terms. Surely it is our job as readers and as teachers to figure out what Huck means when he talks about high-riding drift canoes, skiffs, oars, cordwood, wood yards, wood ranks, wood-flats, flatboats, double-hull ferries, horse ferries, wharfboats, scows, keelboats, thwarts, chutes, crossing, warping, and quartering. To ignore them as we read, or to assume that we can always accurately guess from the context what Huck means by them, is to miss the boat.

CHAPTER FOUR

"Amongst some bundles of shingles"

A Baby, a Barrel, a Home

W HEN *Adventures of Huckleberry Finn* was first published in 1885, it lacked a thirteen-page episode in which Huck swims to a huge lumber raft in the hope of finding out how far ahead Cairo is. Twain had written the episode for the novel, but then he set the unfinished novel aside and worked on other projects. One of those projects was a nonfiction book he called *Life on the Mississippi*. Twain decided that the thirteen-page episode would fit nicely in chapter 3 of this book instead, as an illustration of early Mississippi River commercial culture. After *Life on the Mississippi* was published in 1883, Twain returned to the novel and finished it. When he sent the manuscript of *Huckleberry Finn* to the publisher, he left the thirteen-page episode in its original place. His publisher, however, persuaded him to leave it out of the novel. In this chapter I take up the vexed question of whether modern editions of the novel should restore the episode to its original place in what became chapter 16 of *Huckleberry Finn*.

That thirteen-page account of Huck's visit to the big raft has been referred to by many names: the raft chapter (Mark Twain), the raft episode (Twain, Peter Beidler, Michael Hearn, Kent Rasmussen), the raft passage (David Carkeet; Robert O'Meally; Sculley Bradley, Richard Beatty, and Hudson Long), the raft scene (Lucinda MacKethan), the raftmen episode (Jonathan Arac, Jay Gillette), the raftsman's passage (Thomas Cooley), the raftsmen passage (Bernard DeVoto, Hamlin Hill), the raftsmen's passage (William Manierre, Peter Schmidt, Emory Elliott, Victor Doyno, Robert O'Meally), the raftsmen episode (Michael Powell), the raftsmen's chapter (Robert Hirst), and even the flatboatmen chapter (David Sloane).

Whatever they call the passage, people who read, teach, edit, or write about *Adventures of Huckleberry Finn* have to come to terms with that thirteen-page account of Huck's visit to the huge lumber raft (figs. 4.1 and 4.2).

In the days before steamboats, Twain tells us in *Life on the Mississippi*, commerce on the river was conducted primarily by family-owned keelboats. The keelboats were floated from the upper reaches of the river and its tributaries down to New Orleans, where they were unloaded and then either sold or slowly poled, pushed, winched, rowed, warped, and dragged back upriver. It was tough work that gave rise to tough boatmen:

A voyage down and back sometimes occupied nine months. In time this commerce increased until it gave employment to hordes of rough and hardy men; rude, uneducated, brave, suffering terrific hardships with sailor-like stoicism;

Figure 4.1. John Harley's drawing of the "monstrous long raft" that Huck swims to in chapter 16 (*HF* 107). Huck eavesdrops, hoping that the raftsmen will say something to indicate how far ahead Cairo is. Harley was hired to illustrate *Life on the Mississippi* (1883). He made some effort to suggest the size of the raft but showed only one of the five wigwams described by Huck and none of the sweeps. He also showed the naked Huck swimming alongside the raft (bottom center of picture), about half a dozen raftsmen, bundles of shingles (to the right of the fire), and one of the two flagpoles mentioned by Huck. The function of the little cabin beside the flagpole is not clear. Huck never describes any such structure.

heavy drinkers, coarse frolickers in moral sties like the Natchez-under-the-hill of that day, heavy fighters, reckless fellows, every one, elephantinely jolly, foul-witted, profane; prodigal of their money, bankrupt at the end of the trip, fond of barbaric finery, prodigious braggarts; yet in the main, honest, trustworthy, faithful to promises and duty, and often picturesquely magnanimous. (*LM* 238)

When the proliferation of steamboats gradually put an end to most of the shipping done on keelboats, these rough-and-tough sailors had to seek alternative employment:

But after a while the steamboats so increased in number and in speed that they were able to absorb the entire commerce; and keelboating died a permanent death. The keelboatman became a deck hand, or a mate, or a pilot on the steamer; and when steamer-berths were not open to him, he took a berth on a Pittsburgh coal-flat or on a pine-raft constructed in the forests up toward the sources of the Mississippi. (*LM* 238–39)

TIMBER RAFT.

Figure 4.2. A drawing of a large lumber raft from *Harper's New Monthly Magazine*, March 1858, 452. This precedes Twain's writing of *Huckleberry Finn* by more than a quarter of a century. Is it possible that Twain saw the drawing and used it to help him imagine the raft he had Huck describe in chapter 16? Notice the raftsmen sitting around, as well as the flagpole, the fire, the booze barrel, the four sweeps (two of them manned) at the end of the raft, and the bundles of shingles. That may be a wigwam that some of the raftsmen lean on to the right of the fire. If Twain had seen this drawing, it might have given him the idea for the fiddle playing, singing, and dancing. Also notice the protruding grub stakes visible on the perimeters of the raft.

In *Life on the Mississippi* Twain wrote of his boyhood memories of the mighty rafts that used to glide past Hannibal:

> In the heyday of the steamboating prosperity, the river from end to end was flaked with coal-fleets and timber rafts, all managed by hand, and employing hosts of the rough characters whom I have been trying to describe. I remember the annual processions of mighty rafts that used to glide by Hannibal when I was a boy,— an acre or so of white, sweet-smelling boards in each raft, a crew of two-dozen men or more, three or four wigwams scattered about the raft's vast level space for storm-quarters,—and I remember the rude ways and the tremendous talk of their big crews, the ex-keelboatmen and their admiringly patterning successors; for we used to swim out a quarter or third of a mile and get onto these rafts and have a ride. (*LM* 239)

As the forests were cleared, however, the rafting industry and the jobs it provided also dried up and became the stuff of nostalgic reminiscence.

What is in the raft episode?

Here is the way Twain introduced the raft episode in chapter 3, "Frescoes from the Past," of *Life on the Mississippi*:

> By way of illustrating keelboat talk and manners, and that now-departed and hardly-remembered raft-life, I will throw in, in this place, a chapter from a book which I have been working at, by fits and starts, during the past five or six years, and may possibly finish in the course of five or six more. The book is a story which details some passages in the life of an ignorant village boy, Huck Finn, son of the town drunkard of my time out west, there. He has run away from his persecuting father, and from a persecuting good widow who wishes to make a nice, truth-telling, respectable boy of him; and with him a slave of the widow's has also escaped. They have found a fragment of a lumber raft (it is high water and dead summer time), and are floating down the river by night, and hiding in the willows by day,—bound for Cairo,—whence the negro will seek freedom in the heart of the free States. (*LM* 239)

The raft episode comprises two distinct but overlapping parts. The first is what I call the bragging narrative, where two large inebriated raftsmen strut, posture, prance, and whoop as they boast about how tough and dangerous they are. For example, one of the men starts off this way: "Whoo-oop! I'm the old original iron-jawed, brass-mounted, copper-bellied corpse-maker from the wilds of Arkansaw! Look at me! I'm the man they call Sudden Death and General Desolation!" (*HF* 109). When he is done bragging, another man starts in: "Whoo-oop! Bow your neck and spread, for the kingdom of sorrow's a-coming! Hold me down to the earth, for I feel my powers a-working! whoo-oop! I'm a child of sin, *don't* let me get a start! . . . Whoo-oop! Bow your neck and spread, for the pet child of Calamity's a-comin'!" (*HF* 110).

This part of the raft episode was almost certainly influenced by Twain's reading of Mississippi River Valley travel narratives. In 1810, for example, an early traveler named Christian Schultz described the outlandish boasting of two drunken sailors: "I am a man; I am a horse; I am a team. I can whip any man *in all Kentucky*, by G-d. . . . I am an alligator, half-man, half-horse; can whip any *on the Mississippi*, by G-d."[1] A riverman named Mike Fink was well-known for his exaggerated bragging: "I can out-run, out-dance, out-jump, out-dive, out-drink, out-holler, and out-lick any white thing in the shape o' human that's ever put foot within two thousand miles o' the big Mississip! Whoop!"[2] There is also this early account of a bragging riverman: "I'm the genuine article, tough as bull's hide, keen as a rifle. I can out-swim, out-swar, out-jump, out-drink, and keep soberer than any man at Catfish Bend. I'm painfully ferochus—I'm spiling for some one to whip me—if there's a creeter in this diggin' that wants to be disappointed in trying to do it, let him yell—whoop-hurra!"[3] The bragging in *Huckleberry Finn* between the man who calls himself General Desolation and the man who calls himself Child of Calamity ends when little Davy, by beating them both up, shows that they are both blowhard cowards.

The second part of the raft episode I call the barrel narrative. We have no recognized source for the moving story that a raftsman named Ed tells about a series of events that he had witnessed involving another raftsman, Dick Allbright, and his dead infant son, Charles William Allbright. The first narrative neatly illustrates the "prodigious braggarts" that Twain described in *Life on the Mississippi*. The second does not. Ed is not bragging when he tells the story of a man who killed his son, hid his body in a barrel, buried the barrel in the riverbank, and ran off to be a raftsman. On Dick Allbright's subsequent rafting journeys past that spot, the barrel with the dead baby inside chased Allbright's raft and caused accidents to happen to the other raftsmen. When the raft captain finally brought the barrel aboard and found the baby inside, Dick Allbright picked up the baby's corpse and jumped with it into the river, where he presumably drowned. Neither he nor his son's body was ever seen again. Shortly after Ed finishes his story, the raftsmen discover Huck crouching naked behind some bundles of shingles. When he is asked his name, Huck identifies himself as Charles William Allbright—the name of the dead baby in Ed's story.

There has been little scholarly agreement or editorial consensus about how to handle the raft episode. One recent scholar referred to the issue of whether modern editors should publish the episode in chapter 16 of the novel as a "notorious crux."[4] Fischer and Salamo said that the issue "remains controversial" (*HF* 409). Another scholar wrote, "Twain scholarship has reached no consensus on how the passage should be handled editorially, much less on the meaning of the passage for the novel as a whole. In many ways, the raftsmen's passage is a bit like Huck Finn himself, a kind of outcast child of the parental body of the book."[5] In this chapter I try to give the outcast child a home.

Why was the raft episode not published in the first (1885) edition of *Huckleberry Finn*?

Twain published *Life on the Mississippi* in 1883. A year later he had finished *Huckleberry Finn* and sent it off to be published by his nephew, Charles L. Webster, with the raft episode in its original place in the novel in chapter 16. Twain did not want *Huckleberry Finn* to be published until at least forty thousand copies had been preordered. To hasten the number of preorders, he asked Webster to provide a "canvassing book" with excerpts from the novel. Afraid that readers of the canvassing book would hesitate to order the novel if they knew that part of it had already been published, Twain wrote to Webster on April 14, 1884, "Be particular & don't get any of that *old* matter into your canvassing book—(the *raft* episode)." A week later, on April 21, Webster wrote to Twain suggesting that they drop the raft episode entirely and publish *Adventures of Huckleberry Finn* without it: "The book is so *much* larger than Tom Sawyer[,] would it not be better to omit that old Mississippi matter? I think it would improve it." Twain wrote back immediately, on April 22, "Yes, I think the raft chapter can be left wholly out, by heaving in a paragraph to say Huck visited the raft to find out how far it might be to Cairo, but got no satisfaction. Even *this* is not necessary unless that raft-visit is referred to later in the book. I think it is, but am not certain." On that authority Webster published the novel without the raft episode (*HF* 408).

These letters establish several facts: (1) Twain originally intended to publish *Huckleberry Finn* with the raft episode in its place in what became chapter 16; (2) Twain suggested leaving the raft episode out of the canvassing book, *not* out of the novel; (3) Webster suggested leaving the raft episode out of the novel in order to make the new book closer in length to *The Adventures of Tom Sawyer*; and (4) Twain approved the removal of the raft episode, provided that Webster check to see if there were later references to it and, if there were, to add a paragraph of explanation about Huck's frustrating visit to the big lumber raft.

Fischer and Salamo stated that if Webster had decided it was necessary to "heave in" a paragraph about the visit to the raft, it was "a paragraph which Clemens certainly would have written himself if required" (*HF* 409). Perhaps this is true, but Twain did not say so. Had he meant this, he would presumably have said, "Yes, I think the raft chapter can be left wholly out, but I will have to heave in a paragraph to say Huck visited the raft to find out how far it might be to Cairo, but got no satisfaction. Even *this* is not necessary unless that raft-visit is referred to later in the book. I think it is, but am not certain. Let me know if I need to write that paragraph."

Webster did publish *Adventures of Huckleberry Finn* without the raft episode. He got his way and made the new book closer in length to *Tom Sawyer*—but not much closer. In the Library of America *Mark Twain: Mississippi Writings* edition, the text of *Tom Sawyer* is 206 pages long. With the raft episode, *Huckleberry Finn* would have been an even 300 pages. Removing the raft episode reduces the novel to 287 pages, still eighty-one pages longer than *Tom Sawyer*. Little was gained by the deletion, but, as we will see, much was lost.

If Webster noticed any later references to the raft episode, he made no effort to add a paragraph to explain them or to ask Twain to add it. Given these facts, what are modern editors of *Huckleberry Finn* to do? Do they follow Twain's original intention and restore the raft episode, either in its original place in chapter 16 or in an appendix? Or do they follow Twain's later intention and leave it out, even though it is no longer important or desirable to make the novel closer in length to *Tom Sawyer*? These questions have been hotly debated.

What reasons have modern editors and scholars given for restoring the raft episode to *Huckleberry Finn*?

Adventures of Huckleberry Finn was published without the raft episode for almost six decades after its initial publication. Then a series of scholars and editors began arguing that for various reasons the raft episode belonged in the novel.

The first edition to put the raft episode back into *Huckleberry Finn* was Bernard DeVoto's in 1942. In his introduction he came close to asking for Twain's forgiveness for doing so, and he speculated that Twain did not restore it himself because he was annoyed at the man who suggested that he do so:

> I have done something which many students of American literature have wanted to do, and for which I hope the choleric ghost of Mark Twain will grant me absolution: I have restored the chapter which Mark ripped out of the manuscript and inserted in *Life on the Mississippi*. At one period in the composition of *Huckleberry Finn* he intended to restore it and he must have had his reasons for not doing so, but he does not tell us what they were. An entry in one of his notebooks shows that George W. Cable advised him to restore it and others must have repeated the advice: it is the almost universal feeling of those who love the book that this passage belongs in it. Possibly it was Cable's suggestion that made Mark determine to leave it out. At the time he still resented Cable's offensive piety while they were on their lecture tour, he felt that he had paid Cable more than he was worth for the tour, and he felt a grievance against him for coming down with a contagious disease while a guest in Mark's house. Mark sometimes reached decisions by just such paths, and it may be that annoyance at Cable deprived a masterpiece of one of its organic parts.[6]

DeVoto did not explain how he knew that almost everyone who loved *Huckleberry Finn* believed that the raft episode belonged there, did not offer any solid evidence that Twain refused to put it in simply because Cable suggested that he put it in, and did not specify why he thought the raft episode was an organic part of the novel.

Before long other scholars offered specific evidence that the raft episode enriched the novel. In 1958 Kenneth Lynn wrote that when Twain moved the raft episode from the manuscript of *Huckleberry Finn* and put it into *Life on the Mississippi*, he "improved a good book at the cost of looting his masterpiece of an episode of extraordinary richness, of great beauty and humor." Lynn focused particularly on the relevance to Huck's situation of the Dick Allbright story of "a man who locked up his son, and of a naked child going down the river in search of its father." Lynn saw that story as "a parable of the search for the father and of death by violence and rebirth by water which takes us to the very heart of the novel." He saw Huck's naming himself Charles William Allbright as his identification with the dead baby, but for some reason Lynn thought that Huck had replied "jokingly."[7]

I question several of Lynn's readings. I don't see, for example, that Dick Allbright "locked up his son" or that the son experienced a "rebirth by water." Furthermore, I cannot agree that Huck is making a joke when he identifies himself as Charles William Allbright. The raftsmen do laugh, but this does not mean that Huck is joking. They make fun of Ed's whole narrative, but their laughter does not mean that Ed means to tell a funny story. Surely Huck himself is so caught up in Ed's story of a baby mistreated by a cruel father that he unconsciously blurts out the dead baby's name when he is asked to identify himself. We recall from chapter 6 of *Tom Sawyer* that Huck "slept on doorsteps in fine weather and in empty hogs-heads in wet" (*TS* 45). In the second paragraph of *Huckleberry Finn* Huck tells how he escaped from the widow's fine house and "lit out" for "my sugar hogshead again" (*HF* 1). How could the barrel-sleeping Huck not feel deeply—and seriously—involved with the baby Charles William Allbright in the barrel?

Five decades ago, as a graduate student at Lehigh University in 1966, I wrote a short paper in a graduate seminar on American literary realism. I reworked it a couple of times and then submitted it to *Modern Fiction Studies*, where it eventually was published.[8] I argued there that the raft episode belonged in the novel, mostly because leaving it out left two unexplained gaps in the narrative.

The first gap comes in the second paragraph of chapter 16, which ends with Huck's suggestion that he "paddle ashore the first time a light showed and tell them pap was behind, coming along with a trading scow, and was a green hand at the business, and wanted to know how far it was to Cairo. Jim thought it was a good idea, so we took a smoke on it and waited" (*HF* 106). In the version published without the episode, the next paragraph starts with the statement "There warn't nothing to do now but to look out sharp for the town [Cairo] and not pass it without seeing it" (*HF* 123). There is no explanation for why they stop looking for a shore light that would lead them to information about Cairo and start instead looking for the lights of Cairo itself. With the raft episode back in its original spot, the gap is filled. We learn that Jim has suggested that Huck swim down to the huge raft and eavesdrop on the raftsmen, hoping that they will talk about how far ahead Cairo is. Huck does swim to the big raft and listens, but the raftsmen do not talk—at least not directly—about the location of Cairo. When he is discovered and questioned, Huck manages to escape. When he returns he decides to stay on his and Jim's own raft and just watch for Cairo. The gap is gone.

The second gap also involves information about the location of Cairo. In the second paragraph of chapter 16, Huck and Jim talk about how they will recognize Cairo:

> We talked about Cairo, and wondered whether we would know it when we got to it. I said likely we wouldn't, because I had heard say there warn't but about a dozen houses there, and if they didn't happen to have them lit up, how was we going to know we was passing a town? Jim said if the two big rivers joined together there, that would show. But I said maybe we might think we was passing the foot of an island and coming into the same old river again. (*HF* 106)

Clearly they have no idea how they will know when they are at or past Cairo. In the originally published version without the raft episode, however, just a few pages later Huck suddenly knows: "When it was daylight, here was the clear Ohio water in shore, sure enough, and outside was the old regular Muddy! So it was all up with Cairo!" (*HF* 129).

Without the raft episode we have no explanation of how Huck knows that. With the raft episode restored, however, we know how Huck knows. He has overheard the raftsmen talking about the contrasting waters of the two rivers: "the muddy Mississippi water" and "the clear water of the Ohio" (*HF* 112). And he has heard one of the raftsmen talk about the way the waters of the two rivers stay separated for many miles below Cairo: "you'll find a wide band of clear water all the way down the east side of the Mississippi for a hundred mile or more" (*HF* 113). With the raft episode back in its place, the second gap is filled and Huck's "sure enough" is clear enough.

In 1968, the year my article appeared, William Manierre argued that the raft episode was important because it filled a different kind of gap. Manierre was troubled by the close juxtaposition of two scenes: the one in chapter 15 in which Huck "humbled myself" to Jim (*HF* 105) and the one in chapter 16 in which Huck decides "to paddle ashore at the first light" (*HF* 124) and turn Jim in. "Because there is no adequate provision for the sudden about-face," Manierre wrote, "we are faced with either of two distasteful alternatives: either the preceding [scene] is considerably less significant than our sensibilities tell us it is or Huck's responses have so little permanence as to be themselves unimportant and lacking in meaning." The problem is solved, he said, if we re-store the raft episode, which "nicely separated" these scenes and "gave the much needed impression that a period of time has elapsed between them." In other words, the raft episode "provides the feeling that a suitable length of time has elapsed during which Huck's 'Conscience' has had a chance to work on him."[9]

I am troubled by Manierre's seeing the raft episode as important only be-cause it gives the "impression" of a lapse of time between Huck's recognition of Jim's humanity and his decision, almost immediately afterward, to report Jim to the local authorities as a runaway slave. I would argue that without the raft episode in place, readers will miss an important clue about why Huck suddenly decides to turn Jim in. That clue comes when Davy asks Huck where he came from. Huck replies, and the conversation with the suspicious raftsmen contin-ues, as follows:

> "From a trading scow. She lays up the bend yonder. I was born in her. Pap has traded up and down here all his life; and he told me to swim off here, because when you went by he said he would like to get some of you to speak to a Mr. Jonas Turner, in Cairo, and tell him—"
> "O, come!"
> "Yes, sir, it's as true as the world; Pap he says—"
> "O, your grandmother!"
> They all laughed, and I tried again to talk, but they broke in on me and stopped me.
> "Now looky-here," says Davy; "you're scared, and so you talk wild." (HF 122)

Huck is smart enough to figure out that they could know he is talking "wild" only because he has told them two mutually contradictory statements: that his father has traded up and down that section of the river all his life and that his fa-ther thinks Cairo is downstream. Huck figures out, from their challenging him immediately after he said his father thought Cairo was ahead of them, that Cai-ro is really behind them. Realizing that they have passed Cairo, Huck quickly alters his story: "It's our first trip" (HF 122). It is noteworthy that Huck's origi-nal plan had been to "tell them pap was behind, coming long with a trading scow, and was a green hand at the business and wanted to know far it was to Cairo" (HF 106). It is not clear why Huck does not follow that plan when questioned by Davy but instead tells him that his pap knows that portion of the river well.

When he gets back to his and Jim's own little raft, then, Huck knows that they have drifted past Cairo in the fog. It is curious, however, that Huck does not tell Jim but simply lets him continue to believe that Cairo and freedom are still ahead. Even more curious is that Huck begins to think like a Southerner. When he is north of Cairo he thinks like a Northerner and can go to Jim and "humble myself" to a black man. Yet as soon as he realizes that he is south of Cairo, he begins to think like a Southerner and is troubled by what he calls his "conscience." He decides to do the "right" thing and report to the local authorities that Jim is a runaway slave:

> My conscience got to stirring me up hotter than ever, until at last I says to it, "Let up on me—it ain't too late yet—I'll paddle ashore at the first light and tell." I felt easy and happy and light as a feather right off. All my troubles was gone. I went on looking out sharp for a light and sort of singing to myself. (HF 124)

Without the raft episode in its place we cannot know why Huck, suddenly realizing that he and Jim are now heading not to Cairo and freedom but deeper into slave territory and bondage, sees that they are in even greater danger than before. Jim is in greater danger because he is heading further south and away from the free states, where he might easily be forgiven for running away. Huck is in greater danger because he would be seen as having helped a slave escape his "rightful owner" (HF 124). Huck now sees turning Jim in as the right thing to do and also the only way to save himself. The raft episode, then, not only gives the "impression" of a lapse in time but, more important, explains why Huck decides so suddenly to rat on Jim.

In 1985 the staff of the Mark Twain Papers in the Bancroft Library at the University of California weighed in with a new edition based on years of research. They published their edition of *Huckleberry Finn* with the raft episode restored. In his note on the text, Robert Hirst, the general editor of the Mark Twain Papers, made this curious statement about their reasons for doing so: "The editors of the present text restore the passage, but not because it improves the book. The passage is restored . . . because Mark Twain intended to publish it in *Huckleberry Finn*, but changed his mind *only* to accommodate the publisher's convenience—a decision roughly akin to accepting the publisher's censorship."[10]

A year later Jay Gillette published an article in which he argued that on the contrary the raft episode should be restored to the novel precisely *because* it improves the novel. It does so in part, he said, by giving Jim a greater leadership role, since it is his idea to visit the raft: "Jim said it was such a black night, now, that it wouldn't be no resk to swim down to the big raft and crawl aboard and listen—they would talk about Cairo, because they would be calculating to go ashore there for a spree, maybe . . .; he could most always start a good plan when you wanted one" (*HF* 107). Mostly, however, Gillette defended the restoration of the episode because it is so well written:

> The excellence of the episode, in form and content, leads me to conclude that we should read *Adventures of Huckleberry Finn* with the passage restored to its original position in chapter 16. . . . There are three general features that represent the excellence of the raftsmen episode and therefore support its inclusion in the text. Firstly, the writing is original—it repeats older genre patterns, but surpasses them. . . . Secondly, the writing is imaginative in form and engages the audience in content. . . . Thirdly, the writing vividly characterizes the types it represents. With a minimum of external description (Bob's hat, for example, is simply "all over ribbons"), Mark Twain demonstrates the outlook and action-orientation of the raft workers. . . . Therefore, the episode belongs in the text of *Adventures of Huckleberry Finn*.[11]

Encouraged by the decision of the editors of the 1985 University of California edition to include the raft episode in chapter 16 of *Huckleberry Finn*, in 1988 David Sloane adduced evidence that the novel was improved by it. Although he mistakenly called the large lumber raft a flatboat—an entirely different floating craft—Sloane drew attention to several issues of balance and symmetry:

> A long chapter describing the life of a flatboatman added local color to the front end of the river voyage and balanced chapters showing yokels at the end of the novel. . . . The chapter adds several important effects. First, it gives an overview of characters on a flatboat, parallel, but lower in class and behavior, to the residents of St. Petersburg. . . . Second, the reader receives a full introduction to the river type, moderating the effect of Pap, otherwise the only sample in the early part of

the book of the common man. Since later samples abound, including Boggs and
the yokels at the Phelps Farm, the flatboatmen chapter strengthens the symmetry of the book. . . . The passage also helps Twain move Huck and Jim's raft past
Cairo, Illinois, and the obvious entrance of the Ohio River. . . . Stories of murderers and tall tales show Huck's lies to be merely the currency of society, with
the difference that his lies are directed toward preserving Jim's safety. Thus, as he
leaves the flatboat and returns to Jim on the raft, the stage is set for an expansion
of Huck's ambiguous sense of his relationship to Jim and a further development
of Huck as a defender of Jim despite the "conscience" imposed on him by Miss
Watson's St. Petersburg.[12]

In 1996 Victor Doyno defended the inclusion of the episode on the basis of
the contrasts, parallels, and foreshadowing it provided:

This long episode, with its great emphasis on male competition, deceit, and dis-
trust, paints a comical picture, but one strongly contrasting to our vision of Huck
and Jim's idyllic life isolated on their raft. The quarreling, boasting, and mutual
suspicion on the large raft foreshadow what will happen later, after the king and
duke intrude upon Huck and Jim's raft. The passage's inset story of the mysteri-
ous, haunting barrel creates suspense. The killing of a son and the child's search
for a father figure mirror, in extreme form, some of Huck's recurrent concerns.[13]

In 2003 Peter Schmidt argued that the raft episode belongs in the novel
because it gives us an example of Huck using "black English." After Davy res-
cues Huck and prevents him from being painted blue by the other raftsmen,
Davy asks, "If we let you off this time, will you keep out of these kind of scrapes
hereafter?" Huck replies, "'Deed I will, boss. You try me" (HF 123). By calling
Davy "boss," Schmidt said, Huck echoes Jim's use of the word at the end of the
previous chapter when speaking to Huck: "Well, looky-here, boss, dey's sumf'n
wrong, dey is. . . . Now ain' dat so, boss—ain't it so?" (HF 103). According to
Schmidt, that the captive Huck uses a word "very much expected to be used
by blacks to show deference to whites" shows that he is identifying with the
enslaved Jim. To remove the episode is to rob Twain's readers of the key realization that "only by adding the raftsmen's passage back to its original place . . . can
we make an important observation: Huck decides to turn Jim in immediately
after those moments with the white raftsmen when—for the first time in the
novel—Huck understands his own racial identity to be ambiguous."[14]

What reasons have modern editors and scholars given for not restoring the raft episode to *Huckleberry Finn*?

Many scholars, of course, have rejected all such arguments as valid reasons to publish *Huckleberry Finn* with the raft episode in its original spot after the second paragraph of chapter 16. Three scholars have been especially vehement in arguing against putting the episode back into the novel. In the introduction to his 1962 facsimile edition of the novel as it was first published in America, Hamlin Hill noted with some dismay that two editions had published the raft episode in its original location. Hill admitted that including the episode was "to some extent a merit" because it helped to "initiate the raft-shore dichotomy which is to be vital in the next section of the novel," but he argued strongly that to include the passage constituted unforgiveable literary tampering: "To add the raftsmen passage to the body of Mark Twain's text is a literary tampering as serious as removing the *Walter Scott* passage would be: the former belongs out (good or bad) because Mark Twain left it out and the latter belongs in (good or bad) because Twain put it in."[15]

In 1997 Jonathan Arac questioned Hirst's statement that Charles Webster, in urging Twain to cut the raft episode, had coerced Twain into dropping the episode and thus made him, in Arac's words, "a victim of censorship." Twain, Arac said, was the senior partner in his nephew's publishing house and was "deeply involved in the whole process by which the book moved from his manuscript to his readers." Actually, Twain was not all *that* involved. He left it up to Webster whether to "heave in" a paragraph to fill the gaps left by removing the raft episode, and he eagerly accepted his friend William Dean Howells's offer to do the proofreading of the novel. But Arac was right to question the idea that cutting the raft episode was in any sense coercion or censorship. Twain was willing enough to approve the removal in order to cut production costs and sell more books. It was Twain's decision, freely made.

Less convincing was Arac's comment that nothing would be gained by restoring the raft episode: "I know of no major interpretive argument about *Huckleberry Finn* which depends on the presence, or the absence, of this episode. However excellent in itself, it seems in no way essential to the whole—as Mark Twain originally judged in agreeing to omit it."[16] It is obviously a matter of personal judgment whether the arguments of scholars like DeVoto, Lynn, Manierre, Hirst, Sloane, Gillette, Doyno, and Schmidt are "major interpretive argument[s]" and whether they show that the raft episode is "essential to the whole." The other question that Arac raised—why Twain himself never reissued the novel with the raft episode restored—I discuss below.

The third scholar to object to the reinsertion of the raft episode was Michael Powell, who claimed that "the raftsmen episode was never a part of Mark Twain's script for *Adventures of Huckleberry Finn*, . . . never a part of the narrative order its author prepared for perpetuity: manuscript; typescript; proof; illustration." In fact, it very much *was* part of the manuscript and the typescript, although Powell was right that it never was part of the proof for the novel, since it had been removed before Webster set *Huckleberry Finn* in print.

Powell found it important that "Twain went out of his way in 1884 to absolutely assure forthcoming subscribers to *Huckleberry Finn* that 'NOT a sentence of this book has ever before appeared in print in any form,' capitalizing 'EVERY LINE FRESH AND NEW'—he this-outspokenly had no intention to print the raftsmen episode in *Huckleberry Finn*." That is so, of course, because by the time those advertisements for the book came out, Twain had already agreed not to print the episode and so was eager to capitalize on the decision by emphasizing the freshness of the novel. At first, however, he *had* intended to print the raft episode.

Powell saw the desire of modern "academicians" to reinsert the raft episode as part of a "critical devaluation of Twain as someone who didn't know how to write a book. . . . *The* great American novel was not written accidentally; it neither needs nor wants 'improving.'" I return to that accusation below. Powell continued by lending his support to Hill's accusation of literary tampering.[17]

Was Hill right to say that putting the raft episode back in is a literary tampering analogous to leaving the *Walter Scott* episode out?

I repeat Hill's statement: "To add the raftsmen passage to the body of Mark Twain's text is a literary tampering as serious as removing the *Walter Scott* passage would be: the former belongs out (good or bad) because Mark Twain left it out and the latter belongs in (good or bad) because Twain put it in." No one would object to the last dozen words of that statement. The *Walter Scott* episode absolutely does belong in. No one—not Mark Twain, not Charles Webster, not any present-day scholar or editor—ever suggested removing it. It functions on all sorts of levels: it provides Huck with the history book that he later reads from to Jim, thus setting up the king and the duke episode; it shows Huck's courage in boarding the wreck, his resourcefulness in escaping from it when his and Jim's raft is swept away, and his concern for the safety of the men left aboard he *Walter Scott*; and it shows the greed of the ferryboat owner, who will not attempt a rescue until he knows who is going to pay him. Removing that episode would be far worse than literary tampering; it would be literary butchering.

To take the *Walter Scott* passage out is not analogous to putting the raft episode back in. The first is deleting what Twain wrote and thus leaving serious gaps in the narrative; the other is restoring what Twain wrote and thus filling serious gaps in the narrative. A better analogy would be that *putting* the raft episode back in is like *leaving* the *Walter Scott* episode in: Twain wrote them both for inclusion in the novel. Canceling either one leaves unfilled gaps in the novel.

How can we answer Arac's question about why, if the raft episode belongs in, Twain never reissued *Huckleberry Finn* with it included?

"It is a nagging embarrassment," Arac said, "to the editors' [of the 1985 University of California edition] scholarly scruple that even where he might have tried to bring the passage back, no evidence exists that Twain ever tried to."[18] Arac was surely not the first to wonder why Twain himself did not reissue the novel with the raft passage put back in. We have already seen from the DeVoto quote above that George W. Cable had suggested putting the raft episode back in. In addition, Twain got a letter from a young Iowan named Albert Johannsen, dated March 15, 1890:

> We have been reading your *Life on the Mississippi*, and *Huckleberry Finn* in our "Mark Twain Reading Club" and as Secretary of the club, I have been requested to write to you, in their behalf, and ask how it is that the chapter taken from *Huck Finn* which appears in *Life on the Mississippi* is not in *Huck Finn*. If you will be so kind as to let us know you will confer a great favor upon our Club.

Twain asked his clerk to "please tell him it is too long a story to tell—would require a chapter."[19] It would have been quick and easy for Twain to say "because that chapter would add nothing" or "because I just like chapter 16 better without the raft episode." The answer he did give—"it is too long a story to tell"—suggests that the reasons were many and complex.

An essayist and biographer named E. V. Lucas mentioned the time in 1907 that he had asked Twain about restoring the raft episode, "I asked him why he had never incorporated in *Huckleberry Finn* the glorious chapter about the boasting bargemen which he dropped into *Life on the Mississippi*. His reasons were not too understandable but I gathered that some copyright question was involved" (*HF* 409).[20] We can only speculate on what the copyright question was. Perhaps the problem was that the raft episode had been copyrighted in *Life on the Mississippi* by a different publisher, who was then reluctant to release the rights to Webster. Perhaps the problem was that to reissue the novel with the additional pages would have meant applying for and paying for a new copyright. Perhaps the problem was that including the raft episode would have meant hiring E. W. Kemble to illustrate it, since John Harley's different style of illustrations for *Life on the Mississippi* would have been copyrighted as part of that book.

One issue might simply have been the length of the chapters. The chapters in the 1885 *Huckleberry Finn* range in length from five to thirteen pages in the Fischer and Salamo illustrated edition, the average being eight to nine pages. Chapter 16, at ten pages, was already one of the longer chapters. With the raft episode added, chapter 16 becomes, with the illustrations, fully twice the length of *any* other chapter in the novel. Twain could have split the chapter and renumbered the subsequent chapters, but that would have been messy, especially since Kemble had usually incorporated the chapter numbers with the opening illustrations.

Another issue might have been the badly deteriorated relationship between Twain and Webster. In his autobiography Twain spoke of Webster's having tricked him into signing a contract giving Webster himself full authority to run the company:

> Under the preceding contracts Webster had been my paid servant; under the new one I was his slave, his absolute slave, and without salary. I owned nine-tenths of the business, I furnished all the capital. I shouldered all the losses. I was responsible for everything, but Webster was sole master.... I could no longer give orders as before. I could not even make a suggestion with any considerable likelihood of its acceptance.[21]

Even if Twain had wanted to reissue *Huckleberry Finn* with the raft episode included, his publisher might have refused.

Whatever the real reasons, none of them apply now. Editors no longer need to worry, as Twain did, about making *Huckleberry Finn* shorter, selling more copies, violating copyright issues, or dealing with Charles Webster.

**Was Powell right to suggest that to argue for the
inclusion of the raft episode is to question Twain's judgment
and to think, hubristically, that we can improve on his novel?**

Of course not. Those who want to restore the raft episode seek not to improve
Twain's novel but to present it as Twain had originally wanted it presented.
They seek not to stifle or shout over Twain's voice but to magnify it. To argue
for the inclusion of the raft episode is not at all to argue that Twain did not
know how to write a novel. On the contrary, it is to argue that he *did*, and that
Twain's initial decision to include the raft episode in *Huckleberry Finn* was the
right one. It was Webster who questioned Twain's literary judgment by asking
him to drop the raft episode: "Would it not be better to omit that old Mississippi matter? I think it would improve it."

**Did Charles Webster follow Twain's directives regarding
the removal of the raft episode?**

On April 22, 1884, Twain replied to Webster's question about omitting the "old
Mississippi matter" entirely. As already noted earlier in this chapter, he wrote,
"I think the raft chapter can be left wholly out, by heaving in a paragraph to
say Huck visited the raft to find out how far it might be to Cairo, but got no
satisfaction. Even *this* is not necessary unless that raft-visit is referred to later in
the book. I think it is, but am not certain." Twain apparently trusted Webster,
who was then in possession of the typescript, to decide whether the paragraph
should be added. Webster decided that no such paragraph was necessary. In
fact, there were two later references to the raft visit. The first one Webster noticed and, apparently on his own authority, simply deleted. The second, if he
noticed it at all, he simply ignored.

   The discovery in 1990 of the first half of the manuscript of *Huckleberry Finn*
showed that Twain originally intended to end the raft-episode chapter with
this sentence about his return to his and Jim's small raft: "I swum out and got
aboard, and was mighty glad to see home again" (*HF* 123). In the manuscript
the next chapter began as follows:

   I had to tell Jim I didn't find out how far it was to Cairo. He was pretty sorry.
   There wasn't anything to do now but look out sharp for the town and not pass it
   without seeing it. He said he would be mighty sure to see it because he would be
   a free man the minute he saw it. (*HF* 501)

I take those first two bolded sentences as the first reference to Huck's visit to the big raft. Rather than adding a paragraph explaining that Huck had visited the raft, Webster simply deleted the two lines, scarcely what Twain had asked him to do. The deletion is important. If I am right to suggest that Huck would have figured out from his conversation with Davy that they already had passed Cairo, then his statement to Jim that he did not find out how far ahead Cairo was is only a partial truth. Huck did not find out how far it was to Cairo because Cairo lay miles behind them. Huck knew, but he did not want Jim to know.

The second reference to the raft visit came seven pages later: "When it was daylight, here was the clear Ohio water in shore, sure enough, and outside was the old regular Muddy! So it was all up with Cairo" (*HF* 129). That was a reference to what Huck had learned from the raftsmen about the way the waters of the two rivers did not like to mix. As a result, Ed said, "You'll find a wide band of clear water all the way down the east side of the Mississippi for a hundred mile or more" (*HF* 113).

Scholars who have objected to reinserting the raft episode have done so mostly on the basis of Twain's supposed intention to cut it. His letter shows that he absolutely did not intend to leave a gap in the narrative. If the removal of the raft episode left a gap, he wanted it filled with an added paragraph, presumably something like the one I draft below (shown in boldface). To put it in context, I reproduce the three paragraphs preceding my insertion and the three sentences following it:

We slept most all day, and started out, at night, a little ways behind a monstrous long raft that was as long going by as a procession. She had four long sweeps at each end, so we judged she carried as many as thirty men, likely. She had five big wigwams aboard, wide apart, and an open camp fire in the middle and a tall flag pole at each end. There was a power of style about her. It *amounted* to something being a raftsman on such a craft as that.

We went drifting down into a big bend, and the night clouded up and got hot. The river was very wide and was walled with solid timber on both sides; you couldn't see a break in it, hardly ever, or a light. We talked about Cairo, and wondered whether we would know it when we got to it. I said likely we wouldn't, because I had heard say there warn't but about a dozen houses there, and if they didn't happen to have them lit up, how was we going to know we was passing a town? Jim said if the two big rivers joined together there, that would show. But I said maybe we might think we was passing the foot of an island and coming into the same old river again. That disturbed Jim—and me too. So the question was, what to do? I said, paddle ashore the first time a light showed, and tell them pap was behind, coming along with a trading scow, and was a green hand at the business and wanted to know how far it was to Cairo. Jim thought it was a good idea, so we took a smoke on it and waited.

But you know a young person can't wait very well when he is impatient to find a thing out. We talked it over, and by and by Jim said it was such a black night, now, that it wouldn't be no resk to swim down to the big raft and crawl aboard and listen—they would talk about Cairo, because they would be calculating to go ashore there for a spree, maybe, or anyway they would send boats ashore to buy whiskey or fresh meat or something. Jim had a wonderful level head, for a nigger; he could most always start a good plan when you wanted one.

Well, I done it. I swum to the raft, clumb aboard, hid amongst some bundles of shingles, and listened to what the raftsmen was chawing about. But they never mentioned nothing about Cairo. One of them talked about how the muddy waters of the Mississippi didn't like to mix with the clear waters of the Ohio, and when the Mississippi was on a rise you could still see the line between the two waters a hunderd mile below Cairo, but that warn't no help, so I swum on back to our raft.

I had to tell Jim I didn't find out how far it was to Cairo. He was pretty sorry. There warn't nothing to do now but to look out sharp for the town and not pass it without seeing it. (HF 106–07, 123)

Notice that by "heaving in" one short paragraph containing the information Twain asked Webster to provide, I have filled the two gaps left by the removal of the raft episode: the otherwise unexplained waiting "now" for sight of Cairo and the source of Huck's knowledge about the unmixed river waters below Cairo. But Webster did not write such a paragraph, and he did not signal Twain to do so. The result in the book that Webster published was a botched chapter 16—scarcely what Twain intended and scarcely what modern editors of the novel should insist that readers read.

To reiterate: Twain told Webster to "heave in" a paragraph if there were later references to Huck's visit to the raft. Twain did not tell Webster to remove such references. Webster ignored Twain's directive, however. He added nothing and removed two sentences. If deleting two sentences without the author's approval is not literary tampering, what is? If ignoring the author's directive to add a paragraph is not literary tampering, what is?

So what is an editor to do?

After considering the evidence, in 1974 Lewis Leary concluded that Twain "maimed" the novel by removing the raft episode:

> What then is a beleaguered editor to do? Mark Twain willingly deleted the passage. It was in his manuscript, but his final decision was to leave it out. Yet almost anyone who reads *Adventures of Huckleberry Finn* without it and then with it can discover the narrative better for the episode being where Mark Twain put it first. A critical editor is confronted with the presumptuous possibility of presenting a text of *Huckleberry Finn* which is better than the text which Mark Twain approved.... Or he can back away, leaving a maimed text still maimed. Of this he can be sure; whatever he does, someone will chew him out for having done it.[22]

We have already considered various ways the narrative is better with the raft episode in place. I would like to add four features that readers will miss if we insist that they read not the full novel that Mark Twain sent to Webster but the shorter one that Webster published.

First, readers will miss the point of the opening paragraph of chapter 16 describing the monstrous long raft that floats along ahead of Huck and Jim's little raft. We know why that paragraph is there if Huck visits the big raft. Why would Twain have included the paragraph at all if Huck was not going to swim down to the raft, climb aboard it, and hear the bragging raftsmen and the Dick Allbright story? That opening paragraph serves no function whatever without the episode it introduced. It becomes just an irrelevant distraction.

Second, readers will miss what Huck learns about manhood and courage when little Davy challenges the bragging and cowardice of Sudden Death and General Desolation and of Child of Calamity. Davy is smaller than either of those big show-offs, does no bragging, and handily whips them both. Huck also learns something about manhood in Ed's story about Dick Allbright when the raft captain puts the cowering raftsmen to shame by diving overboard to bring the barrel back to the raft. Those lessons in manhood provide an introduction to the stalwart but destructive manhood of the Grangerfords and the

Shepherdsons in chapter 18 and to the bold but merciless manhood of Colonel Sherburn when he disperses the mob of cowards who set out to lynch him in chapter 22.

Third, readers will miss the psychological relevance of Huck's giving as his own name Charles William Allbright, the name of the murdered baby in Ed's story about the haunted barrel. Huck had earlier staged his own death when he escaped his pap's log shanty in such a way that it would look as if he had been murdered. A few days later Huck learns from Mrs. Loftus that the people of St. Petersburg believed that Huck had been murdered by his father: "people thinks now that he killed his boy and fixed things so folks would think robbers done it, and then he'd get his hands on Huck's money" (*HF* 69–70).

Not long after, Huck overhears Ed's moving story of Dick Allbright's being pursued by a murdered baby in a floating barrel. Allbright finally confesses that he had killed his baby: "He said he used to live up at the head of this bend, and one night he choked his child, which was crying, not intending to kill it, which was prob'ly a lie" (*HF* 118). Huck must have wondered whether the baby in the barrel was pursuing his father because he wanted to get revenge or because he wanted his father to acknowledge his existence by taking him in his arms again. Perhaps trying to assure himself that he is not the cold, stiff, and naked dead baby in the barrel, Huck says that he is "warm and soft and naked" (*HF* 120). But when asked to identify himself, Huck blurts out the name of the dead baby. Then, perhaps unconsciously echoing the language of Dick Allbright, he says that he lived with his father "up at the head of the bend" (*HF* 122). It is surely no mere joke or irrelevant lie that, naked as the day he was born, Huck identifies himself as the murdered son of a cruel father.

With the raft episode removed, we miss the opportunity to speculate on why Huck, having been abused by his own father, takes on the name Charles William Allbright.[23]

Fourth, the absence of the raft episode also means that readers will miss the significance of Huck's statement at the very end: "When Jim come along by and by, the big raft was away out of sight around the point. I swum out and got aboard, and was mighty glad to see **home** again" (*HF* 123). Huck is searching for home throughout the novel. He does not find it in "my sugar hogshead" (*HF* 1). He does not find it in the Widow Douglas's house, which he escapes as quickly as he can. He surely does not find it in his pap's log shanty, which he also escapes the first chance he gets. He finds something he briefly calls home on Jackson's Island with Jim. "We got **home** all safe," Huck says after he and Jim visit the floating house (*HF* 62). Only a few days later, however, when that island home is invaded by runaway-slave catchers, Huck is forced to make still another escape, this time on the little raft and this time with Jim. Like his earlier homes, this one he is also forced to abandon, when it is struck by a steamboat: "all of a sudden she bulged out, big and scary, with a long row of wide-open furnace-doors shining like red-hot teeth, and her monstrous bows and guards hanging right over us" (*HF* 130).

Huck's search for a home continues to be frustrating. He is impressed by the Grangerfords—"a mighty nice family, and a mighty nice house" (*HF* 136). He appreciates their offer—"they said I could have a **home** there as long as I wanted it" (*HF* 135)—but the offer is soon rendered meaningless by the murderous feud with the Shepherdsons. The raft again becomes Huck's home, but it is soon invaded by the dangerous "royal" charlatans, who in their desperate greed sell Jim off. The Phelps place also proves to be unsatisfactory as a home to the perennially homeless Huck, who decides to light out for the Territory rather than make a home with Tom's Aunt Sally: "She's going to adopt me and sivilize me and I can't stand it. I been there before" (*HF* 362). For Huck and Jim, home is where their raft is: "We said there warn't no **home** like a raft, after all. Other places do seem so cramped up and smothery, but a raft don't. You feel mighty free and easy and comfortable on a raft" (*HF* 155).

To be deprived of the raft episode, then, is to be deprived of an important epiphany in the novel: Huck's realization that the raft is his home and that he is "mighty glad to see **home** again" (*HF* 123). Huck is a bit like a lumber crib separated from its parent raft. He thinks he will find direction from the raftsmen on the big raft, but what he finds is a fearsome story about a boy murdered by his father and buried in a barrel. The barrel narrative must have made him see that the sugar hogshead he once called home was more like a coffin than a home. In the raft episode, instead of finding emancipating information, Huck finds information that lets him know that he and Jim have left freedom far behind them in Cairo. On the "monstrous long raft" (*HF* 106) he finds threatening monsters. He happily returns to his crib, his little section of a lumber raft, where he finds himself the closest he will come in the novel to a meaningful parent and a meaningful home. Do we really want to let Webster's deletion of "mighty glad to see home again" stand?

CHAPTER FIVE

"Generally known as a ˈsucker"

A Boy, a Raft, a River

IN THE FALL of 1863 a fourteen-year-old Wisconsin boy named Ceylon Childs Lincoln enlisted in the Union Army. His three brothers all eventually died in the Civil War, but he survived. After the war ended, Lincoln worked as a printer for a while. Then in 1868, when he was eighteen, he signed on as a raftsman on a lumber raft originating in Stevens Point, Wisconsin. Its destination was St. Louis, Missouri. In this closing chapter I reproduce a report that Lincoln gave four decades later about his rafting experience. His report was given orally at the October 20, 1910, meeting of the State Historical Society of Wisconsin, then published in the 1911 proceedings of the society.[1] I reproduce it here in its entirety, including the three footnotes supplied by the editors of the proceedings. I do so primarily because the report helps us answer two questions about *Huckleberry Finn*. First, how might we explain the sudden appearance of the little section of a lumber raft that offered itself as an escape vehicle to Huck and Jim? Second, how might we explain the strange behavior of the raftsmen that Huck observed when he swam to the monstrous lumber raft in chapter 16?

Lincoln's trip had two parts. The first started at a sawmill in Stevens Point, a city in central Wisconsin on the Wisconsin River. From there the Wisconsin River flowed south and then west to Bridgeport, where it emptied into the Mississippi River. This part of the trip was the most dangerous because the Wisconsin River was narrow in places, shallow in places, and obstructed by many rapids, rocks, dams, and bridges. The Wisconsin River passed through many locations that challenged even the most experienced raftsmen. To get through the Wisconsin River portion of the trip, the cribs were fastened together end to end into rapids pieces of six, seven, or more cribs. These long and narrow rapids pieces had two large steering oars, one at the front of the lead crib in the string and one at the rear of the last crib. Generally two oarsmen could manage a rapids piece by themselves, but sometimes, for certain particularly treacherous rapids or dams, they needed to park some pieces at the start of the obstruction and put larger crews on the foremost piece. There would still be only the one steering oar at the front and one at the rear, but instead of one raftsman pushing on it, there would be two, three, four, or even five men pushing on it. Once past the obstruction, they would tie the piece to the riverbank and then gig, or slog, back along the bank upstream to bring another rapids piece down. Once the rapids pieces were all successfully through that obstruction, the raftsmen would return to their original rapids pieces and proceed downstream to the next dam or rapids.

Much could go wrong on the Wisconsin River. If there was too much flow because of rain or melting snow, the raftsmen could not steer their rafts with anything like precision. A more serious problem was that there was often too little water flow to carry the rapids pieces over the rocks.

When a town or a business built a dam across the river, it had to provide an overflow slide that was wide enough to permit rapids pieces to make their way down the river, but the slide required a certain volume of water. Not all cribs or rapids pieces made it down the Wisconsin River in a given season. In a dry year the water level in the river might be so low that it shortened the rafting season. If that were the case, then some rapids pieces might get trapped upstream and have to wait until the next season for the trip out. By the next season, after a full year in the water, these flood-trash rafts, as they were called, were slower, heavier, deeper in the water, more likely to hit bottom, more difficult to steer, and more difficult to dislodge when they ran aground on a rocky river bottom or a sandbar.

Once Lincoln's raft got past the worst of the rapids, the river widened and the raftsmen set out on the second part of the journey to St. Louis. They yoked several of the rapids pieces together into larger Wisconsin rafts. As the Wisconsin rafts came into the wider Mississippi River, they were themselves joined together into a Mississippi raft, covering an acre or more. In this part of their journey there was less danger for the raftsmen, but there was still plenty for them to do. Instead of floating only during daylight hours and resting all night, they now floated both day and night. Instead of being challenged mostly by rapids, dams, and rocks, they had to watch out for sandbars, submerged trees, treacherous crosswinds, and steamboats.

When they got to St. Louis, the raftsmen were paid. They found plenty to spend their wages on in St. Louis before they returned home.

Personal Experiences of a Wisconsin River Raftsman by Ceylon Childs Lincoln[2]

The process of making rafts for descending Wisconsin River was as follows: There were secured some hundreds of white-oak grubs that had been dug up ("grubbed") by the roots. These were then shaved down to two inches in diameter, with a knob at one end, and the other sharpened, leaving the whole about three feet in length. Two planks, twelve inches wide by sixteen feet long, were bored at each end and in the middle, to receive these grubs. Placed at a proper distance apart, the lumber was laid on in alternate courses until twelve to sixteen courses were thus placed. The upper binder planks were then put on, parallel with those underneath, and the grubs tightly fastened through them. This formed what was called a crib. Six or seven of these cribs, fastened together longitudinally, were known as a "rapids piece." The latter was then furnished with an eight-inch square timber at bow and stern, with a two-inch oar-pin in the centre of each.

A bow- and tail-oar completed the equipment. These latter were very large, the stems thirty feet long, one foot in diameter at one end, at the other tapering nearly to a point. The blade of the oar (usually sixteen to eighteen feet long, six-teen inches wide, and tapering from three to one inch in thickness) was inserted in the larger end of the stem. The whole was then hung balanced on the oar-pin. It took an expert to handle such an oar so as to give power to the stroke. A begin-ner (generally known as a "sucker") made laughable work trying to acquire the art of dipping such oars. He usually had to breast them around, until he learned bet-ter. To do good service with one of these oars, it must be dipped with one hand and swung above the head at arm's length, then surged upon with every step.

A "fleet"

After these rapids pieces were made and coupled together, they were loaded down with shingles or lath, until they floated about two courses out of the water. A number of such rapids pieces (as many as thirty or forty) constituted a fleet, and contained as much as a million feet of lumber, besides the lath and shingles.

These fleets were run to market either by a contractor or by the milling company itself. If there were cribs enough to make what are called ten "Wisconsin rafts," a pilot and steersman, ten bowsmen and ten tailsmen are engaged as a fleet crew. The bowsmen must be experienced in running the river, their wages from Stevens Point being about $90 for the trip; while the tails-men receive $60. The time occupied might be three weeks or six. A cook and skiffsman were also employed; and in running all dams and rapids, extra pilots and steersmen were hired. The crew was run in two shifts, five men at each bow- and stern-oar.

Fleets of lumber that had started the year before but failed to get down during high water were attempted the second year. These were known to the rivermen as "flood trash," since they were water-logged and floated low and run slowly. The fleets of new timber always had the right of way.

Dangerous rapids and dams

The dangerous places on the Wisconsin were Big and Little Bull Falls, Stevens Point dam, Conant Rapids, Grand Rapids, Clinton's big and little dams, Whitney Rapids, the Dells, and Kilbourn dam. The Mosinee (Little Bull) rapids were the most dangerous on the river, which here narrows to not more than thirty feet in width and plunges down a gulch thirty feet deep, with solid rock wall on either side. The rapids, about half a mile long, are a seething mass of foam and waves. When the rapids piece entered this place, a line was stretched the whole length of the raft, called the "sucker line," which each man seized—for quite often the raft dove ten to twenty rods at a time, and all that could be seen of the men above the water was their heads, and sometimes not even these were in sight.

An early experience

My first experience in rafting was in 1868, when I went down with Homer Chase of Stevens Point as pilot—a first class man. Being a sucker, I was unfortunately hired to make the trip on a flood-trash fleet, belonging to Walter D. McIndoo.

The ice went out of the river April 17, and the next day we started with five men at each oar, to run the Stevens Point dam, near which the lumber had lain throughout the winter. The first trip for a sucker made his hair stand on end, and brought to his mind all the misdeeds of his past life.

We ran down the centre of the river, until within twenty rods of the dam. There the current drew off to the right and came in between two piers, about thirty feet apart; between these piers was the slide, constructed of long logs (called "fingers") fastened with chains to the dam; on either side of the slide, the water dropped about fifteen feet.[3] Below the dam, the river boiled and rolled into whitecaps. If one was fortunate enough to make the slide properly, he could make his landing in the right place; otherwise, there was great danger of saddlebagging one of the piers and breaking to pieces. Sometimes the raft turned a complete somersault, and the men who did not leap for the pier were drowned. Even when going over the slide, our rafts generally sank until we were standing waist-deep in the water, bumping along on the rocks.

Our fleet was made up of twenty-seven rapids pieces, which when coupled together, three abreast, made nine Wisconsin River rafts. It took twenty-seven trips to get our fleet over each dam and rapids, fourteen for each crew of twelve men, and made a great deal of gigging.[4] After running over some of the rapids we had to walk, or rather go on a dog-trot, five miles with our clothes wet and our shoes full of sand, and be there on time when the piece was set loose.

The next obstacle below Stevens Point was Conant Rapids. There the river makes a big double turn to the right. At the second bend is a large red rock, projecting out of the water about a foot. To make the run here, the bow oar must be pulled several strokes to the right, while the steersman pulled the reverse, and as the raft turned, the tail would just slide over the rock. As soon as you passed this rock, the raft dove through the "hog hole"—a place where the water draws between rocks and dives down ten feet or more and then rolls back. These were fearful-looking places to run. The men usually stepped back behind the oars and grabbed the sucker line, and the pilot and steersman held down their oars to keep them from striking on rocks, and being knocked from their hands. Often a wave caught them, and swung them sideways, sweeping some of the men into the river. This was a place where many lives were lost.

The next place to be reached was called Bean Pot Eddy, where the water resembles beans boiling in a kettle. Here the raft sank under water and ran that way for about twenty rods, bumping over rocks. It was about three miles through Conant Rapids, and a very long gig had here to be made.

The Grand Rapids were the next place of importance. It is a sight to stand on shore and see a raft coming down these rapids, between the piers and rocks, the waves rolling, and the foam and mist flying. Although about a mile in length, it only took three or four minutes to make the trip, and the pilot and steersman must make no wrong turns. Just below Grand Rapids bridge there is an eddy where I have seen rafts come to a complete standstill; and below that and just to the left of the river's centre was the Sugar Bowl, a large rock on which many rafts were wrecked.

Below Grand Rapids we come to Clinton's big and little dams, only about thirty rods apart. The large dam is run close to the right-hand shore, and as we passed over it the pilot pulled hard to the left and the steersman the reverse, in order to swing the raft and make the crossing as soon as possible. The distance is so short that one must do rapid work. Just below the lower dam at the right are two large rocks projecting about three feet out of the water and twenty feet across. Not a few rafts saddlebag on these rocks.

Once when passing here, our second crew overtook us, and at the first dam their bow locked our stern so as to render two oars useless. At the second dam we broke away from them, and in the confusion brought up sideways against the first rock, doubled against it, and partly sank. Some of the men made the rock, while others floated away on bunches of shingles. The other rapids piece saddlebagged the second rock. We were there all day before a skiff took us off, and had a fine opportunity to watch the rapids pieces come over the dams. Scarcely one that did not lose lumber, shooting out from behind. Some men made a business of taking station just below all bad places, in order to pick up loose lumber and shingles that floated to them. In time they would get together enough to make a raft, and then would float it down the river to sell.

Whitney Rapids came next, not difficult to run. Just below them we tied up at Point Bas. There three rapids pieces were coupled side by side to make a Wisconsin River raft. All the oars were unshipped save the centre bow- and tail-oars. This first trip, we had nine Wisconsin rafts; the pilot then took charge of the first raft and all followed, the cook shanty being placed on the last.

The first day's run after this was past Grignon's Bend, a long, continuous reach where a sucker first pulled an oar alone. This was the hardest day's work of his life, for it was a steady pull to keep away from the banks, as the water in a bend draws against the bank. If the tail was allowed to strike, the bow was thrown in, and bucked, or swung, which was liable to break the raft to pieces.

Our fleet, being water-soaked lumber, floated low and slowly, and before we reached Portage we were hung up on several sandbars, and had to do handspiking.

We ran the Dells without accidents; but when we came to the Devil's Elbow, I thought the river had come to an end. This was a very difficult place. The pilot pulled two strokes to the left, and then the tail-oar two to the right, and then these strokes were immediately reversed. A notched rock lies just left of the second bend, and if the bow of the raft struck this, it was sure to double under, swing across the river, and break in two.

Drifting over sandbars

After the dangers and trials from rapids and dams came the tedious drifting over sandbars. If one of the head rafts crossed too high or too low to keep the channel, it would ground on a bar, and the next raft would throw the men a line and try and pull it off. Oftentimes they only succeeded in swinging the second raft on to the same or a neighboring bar, until several would be hung up close together. Then the rest of the rafts would tie up, and the men be sent back to help handspike off the stationary rafts. If this proved impossible, we would uncouple two or three strings and let them float around, until the others could be handspiked loose.

Each of us had to get into the water. There was no hanging back; if one did not jump right in, he was pushed in. Sometimes the rafts moved off before a man could catch on, and he would be in water up to his neck. Men worked that way for days, with no way to dry their clothes. I remember that we were in sight of Portage, handspiking for several days before we were able to pass the town.

We seldom had the chance to go to the raft on which the cook shanty was placed, for our meals. Our food was brought alongside of us by a small skiff that accompanied the fleet. The fare was very good, considering the way in which it was served.

We never floated down at night, but each raft tied up, with a half-inch cable to the bank. When our day's work was finished, we would run the raft close to the bank; the tailsman would jump ashore and make the end of the rope fast with a hitch, while the bowsman secured it on the raft itself. Our rope being old, often broke; then we would ground by shoving a plank down between the pieces until it scraped the bottom and checked the momentum.

There were but few bridges across the river at this time. Those there were, we ran without the aid of a pilot, as a man was generally stationed to give us directions how to steer through the piers.

Our fleet was loaded with newly sawed shingles, most of which were unloaded and sold at what was then called Upper Sauk Town. There was quite a traffic in shingles during the night. There would come a dip of oars, and a skiff would draw alongside the raft, and want to trade whiskey for shingles. It was surprising to see what a lot of shingles it took to purchase a quart of poor whiskey!

On the Mississippi

When our fleet arrived at the mouth of the river there was great rejoicing, as the hard work was mostly over. The nine Wisconsin rafts were coupled into one large Mississippi raft, with the cook shanty in the middle, and a long table where men could be seated at meals. Our Mississippi raft consisted of three Wisconsin rafts abreast and three deep, making a raft 144 feet wide and 380 long. There were nine bow-oars and the same number of tail-oars, and we generally ran night and day.

I remember that one day the wind blew hard and drove the raft close to the left bank, where it took all the force, hard pulling from dawn till dark, to keep from bucking the shore and swinging around. Just at night we managed to cross to the right bank. The wind, coming in our rear, drove us forward at what seemed a mile a minute. We sent our skiff, with two men and a rope, to try and fasten us up, and we payed out from the raft nearly a thousand feet of line; but we did not even check her course, and the rope soon broke.

Having pulled all day at the oars, the men had gloomy fears of continuing all night. The pilot, however, steered for what he thought was a slow slough; and although we partly saddlebagged an island, we finally swung into it, the rear end sliding over young trees. Just as we were emerging into the main river, a large tree was leaning over the water, and as the raft struck this we snubbed her dead with the rope, and were tied up for the night.

We lay there for three days waiting for the wind to go down, but the supposed slough proved to be the main steamboat channel, for many boats passed us as we lay there.

The scenery along the Mississippi in June was beautiful—farms sloping down to the river, and city succeeding city. The rapids at Rock Island, with the railroad bridge, made a beautiful picture. We ran the bridge just at dusk, when it was alight with lanterns of different colors. The Quincy bridge was likewise a fine piece of workmanship.

Finally we reached Alton, where we tied up and awaited orders from St. Louis. We could not cross to the west side, because of a high west wind. One night I was on watch, and having strict orders to call the pilot if the wind subsided, I aroused him about sunrise. Soon we were under way, and reached St. Louis about noon. There were large snubbing-works, with windlasses and two-inch cables, at which to tie up all rafts. Of these there were so many that we lay almost in the centre of the river.

They sent out to us a new rope, with orders to snub her dead on the raft, and they would let out from shore. We failed to hold, as they did not give us enough line. Our snubbing apparatus consisted of a large log lying across a second, both pinned fast. As the rope wound round this block, men poured pails of water on it to keep it from catching fire by friction.

Having missed our landing, our pilot was in a dilemma. As we had floated for some distance, he hailed a steamboat, whose captain agreed to push us back for $100. The raft was then partly uncoupled, and the vessel tried to come in between the parts; but missing this, the captain backed her off, and then coming ahead struck the raft on its side, and pushed it to shore, this was done so fast that the tiers next shore doubled under. The vessel held the raft against the shore until we could get several lines made fast. Then what rejoicing, to know we had fairly landed! Then and there we pledged ourselves never to make another trip on old flood trash.

Having received my $60 check, I was escorted by a man awaiting the chance, to a clothing store, and then to see the town. Soon, however, our tickets were purchased for home, where I arrived with but $8 left for sixty days of the hardest work I ever knew.

What does Lincoln's report tell us about the possible origins of the little segment of a lumber raft that Huck and Jim "catched" and took ownership of?

It tells us that their raft was not one of the flood-trash rafts that Lincoln helped to steer. Huck and Jim's raft was made of "nice pine planks," and "the top stood above the water six or seven inches" (*HF* 60). If it had been a flood-trash raft, the planks would have been discolored and the crib would have ridden lower in the water. We can never know precisely what catastrophe caused this particular crib to be separated from the rapids piece it must have once been part of, but it is important to note that it came to Huck and Jim during flood times: "The river went on raising and raising for ten or twelve days, till at last it was over the banks. The water was three or four foot deep on the island in the low places and on the Illinois bottom" (*HF* 60).

Because of the higher than usual flood levels, we can probably assume that the rushing waters of the river and its tributaries farther upstream caused the rapids piece, or the larger raft that it had been part of, to crash into a dam, a bank, a rock, or another raft. If the Mississippi River was that high as far south as St. Petersburg, it must have been fed by real gushers up in the headwaters, where the lumber cribs were assembled. Normally only the first and last crib on a rapids piece had a steering oar, so that this one had two steering oars was unusual, suggesting that someone else had caught this crib, mounted shorter than usual sweeps on its fore and aft middle grub stakes, and then failed to secure the raft to a reliable snub. The force of the river current and the rising floodwaters then brought to Huck and Jim a lucky drift crib with two sweeps already in place.

Another possibility is that Huck and Jim's raft had been made up of lumber collected below a particularly bad place on the Wisconsin River, like this one below the two Clinton dams near Grand Rapids. Lincoln mentioned two large rocks just after the second dam that were often struck by rapids pieces:

> At the second dam we broke away from [another raft], and in the confusion brought up sideways against the first rock, doubled against it, and partly sank. Some of the men made the rock, while others floated away on bunches of shingles. The other rapids piece saddlebagged the second rock. We were there all day before a skiff took us off, and had a fine opportunity to watch the rapids pieces come over the dams. Scarcely one that did not lose lumber, shooting out from behind. Some men made a business of taking station just below all bad places, in order to pick up loose lumber and shingles that floated to them. In time they would get together enough to make a raft, and then would float it down the river to sell.

It is possible that Huck and Jim's raft was made of lumber torn loose from several rapids pieces in just such a spot. The planks were salvaged by the wood collectors, who then outfitted the new raft with a set of small steering oars. Perhaps they failed to secure the raft carefully one night, making it possible for rising waters to carry it off and for Huck and Jim to claim it. We can never know, of course, because Huck does not tell us, but Lincoln's account makes it easy to understand the several ways that their small raft could have become separated from its parent raft.

How does the size of Lincoln's Mississippi raft compare with the "monstrous" raft that Huck visits in chapter 16?

It is impossible to be precise, because Huck is not, but Huck does report that the "monstrous long raft" (*HF* 106) that he visited had four sweeps at either end. This means that the raft was four cribs wide. Lincoln's raft, in contrast, was nine cribs wide and so had nine sweeps at either end. As for the length, Huck says only that it was "as long going by as a procession" (*HF* 106). Lincoln was more precise in his figures. The Mississippi raft he served on was 144 feet wide and 380 feet long. That meant the surface area was almost 55,000 square feet, or a little more than an acre and a quarter. The monster raft that Huck visited was probably no more than half an acre in surface area—monstrously huge in Huck's eyes, but not so very big by Mississippi standards.

What does Lincoln's report tell us about the strange behavior of the raftsmen on the monstrous big raft in chapter 16?

It tells us that they had just been through an unusually swift and dangerous downriver run. The high floodwaters suggest that they had probably experienced a frighteningly fast-paced descent from the upper reaches of a narrow river and had gone roaring over dams and rapids. They had almost certainly spent part of the journey underwater, holding for dear life onto a sucker line. They might have lost one of their fellow raftsmen when his steering oar bumped into a rock or a wave swept him off the raft. They were probably aware that they were lucky to be alive and to have a chance to relax now that they were on the Mississippi River.

Is it any wonder that Huck thinks the raftsmen he meets are "a mighty rough looking lot"? Rafting was tough and dangerous work. It is not surprising that when they finally get a chance to relax, they get drunk: "They had a jug, and tin cups, and they kept the jug moving" (*HF* 107). After reading Lincoln's report, we might wonder whether these raftsmen had surreptitiously traded shingles they did not own for whiskey. We cannot know, but after what they had probably been through, it is easy enough to understand that they felt jittery, wanted to get drunk, and needed to brag to one another about a bravery they did not feel so sure of. And it is easy to understand why they would be suspicious of a naked boy who suddenly appeared among them claiming to bear the name of the dead baby in the barrel that Ed had just told them about.

Just after Ed has told the spooky story of Dick Allbright and the haunted barrel, the other raftsmen, perhaps to conceal their own unease, make fun of him:

Then they all haw-hawed.

"Say, Edward, don't you reckon you'd better take a pill? You look bad—don't you feel pale?" says the Child of Calamity.

"O, come, now, Eddy," says Jimmy, "show up; you must a kept a part of that bar'l to prove the thing by. Show us the bunghole—*do*—and we'll all believe you."

"Say, boys," says Bill, "less divide it up. Thar's thirteen of us. I can swaller a thirteenth of the yarn, if you can worry down the rest."

Ed got up mad and said they could all go to some place which he ripped out pretty savage, and then walked off aft cussing to himself, and they yelling and jeering at him and roaring and laughing so you could hear them a mile.

"Boys, we'll split a watermelon on that," says the Child of Calamity, and he come rummaging around in the dark amongst the shingle bundles where I was, and put his hand on me. I was warm and soft and naked; so he says "Ouch!" and jumped back.

"Fetch a lantern or a chunk of fire here, boys—there's a snake here as big as a cow!"

So they run there with a lantern and crowded up and looked in on me.

"Come out of that, you beggar!" says one.

"Who are you?" says another.

"What are you after here? Speak up prompt, or overboard you go."

"Snake him out, boys. Snatch him out by the heels." (*HF* 119–20)

It is probably going too far to suggest that Huck is in a sense reborn, in a kind of breech birth, but the hints are all here: the story of a dead baby, the alarmed raftsmen (midwives) reaching for a watermelon (the baby's head), the snake (the umbilical cord), and the baby being pulled out by the heels (breech birth). If the concept of a rebirth works here at all, it is a rebirth into a world in which Huck realizes that the "monstrous long raft" is not a place he can find a home, any more than Charles William Allbright could.

Like Huck Finn and Ceylon Lincoln, we have reached the end of our journey. At the end of his journey, Huck lights out for the Territory. At the end of his journey, Lincoln took his eight dollars and headed back to Stevens Point,

Wisconsin. At the end of our journey, we head back to St. Petersburg ready to start down the mighty Mississippi River with Huckleberry Finn once again. This time, however, we will have better answers to our questions about the river and the rafts and other rivercraft on it. When we read that Huck and Jim catch a little section of a lumber raft, we will know what they have caught, and we will know that it almost certainly was built from the sawed lumber of *Pinus strobus* white pine trees cut down in Wisconsin. We will know that protruding from the raft's surface are grub stakes secured by hardwood wedges called witches.

We will know what the wigwam that Jim built looks like. We will know what the two steering oars, also known as sweeps, look like, and why two of them are required to move the raft sideways to keep it in the current that provides the main means of moving the raft. Because we will understand that it was sometimes difficult to check, or snub, a raft being pushed along by a swift current, we will know why Jim on his raft becomes separated from Huck in his canoe.

We will understand what kind of canoe Huck has and how it differs both in looks and in means of locomotion from the skiff that the two slave traders row when they talk to Huck and from the yawl that the king and the duke, pretending to be the English brothers of Peter Wilks, are carried ashore in from the steamboat.

We will understand that the steamboat's boilers are fueled by wood supplied by wood yards that store firewood in wood ranks along the riverbanks. We will understand that upstream boats sometimes took in tow large barges known as woodboats or wood-flats that were unloaded as the steamboat steamed upriver, then cut adrift to float back down the river to the wood yard, where they were filled up again for the next upriver steamboat. We will know what a horse ferry is and what a wharfboat is.

We will know that Huck is not the first raftsman to lie about the presence of a smallpox victim on his raft. And we will know why Twain wrote the raft episode and why we should restore it to its original place in chapter 16. With the raft episode back where it belongs, we not only understand something about the big raft that Huck's little raft was once part of, we also understand why Huck, like Charles William Allbright, cannot return to his old home or rejoin the father who once abused him. Charles William Allbright had come home to the raft to find his father, only to discover that their reunion would mean forcing his father to join him in death. Huck, in contrast, finds life through rebirth as the son of a new father. Reborn, Huck returns to the crib that has become his home. By identifying the man on the crib with him as white, Huck saves not only Jim but also himself by his realization that Jim is, in his eyes, no longer a black man but a human being.

In conclusion, we will start our next journey downriver with Huck and Jim knowing the answers to all sorts of historical, nautical, technical, and psychological questions. Surely modern-day readers of *Huckleberry Finn* owe it to the author of one of the most widely read, most universally admired, and most superficially understood American novels to immerse themselves in the culture of the rafts and other rivercraft that are so important to an understanding and appreciation of the novel. It has been the purpose of this book to steer such readers back to the main channel.

Notes

Introduction

1. R. Kent Rasmussen, *Critical Companion to Mark Twain: A Literary Reference to His Life and Work* (New York: Facts on File, 2007), 198; Andrew Levy, *Huck Finn's America: Mark Twain and the Era That Shaped His Masterpiece* (New York: Simon and Schuster, 2015), 201–2.

2. Mark Twain, *Adventures of Huckleberry Finn (Tom Sawyer's Comrade)*, ed. Victor Fischer and Lin Salamo (Berkeley: University of California Press, 2001), xlv. Subsequent page numbers, preceded by "*HF*" and given in parentheses, refer to this edition. The novel was first published in the United States in 1885.

3. David Carkeet, "The Dialects in *Huckleberry Finn*," *American Literature* 51 (1979): 315–32.

4. Mark Twain, *Life on the Mississippi*, in *Mark Twain: Mississippi Writings* (Berkeley, CA: Library of America, 1982), 290, 292. Subsequent page citations of *Life on the Mississippi*, placed after "*LM*" in parentheses, are from this edition. *Life on the Mississippi* was originally published in 1883. Twain never used the term *timber raft* in *Huckleberry Finn*. He used the term *timber*, but only to refer to trees before they were cut down.

Chapter One

1. Lee Smith, *The Last Girls: A Novel* (New York: Ballantine Books, 2002), xi. Although *The Last Girls* is a work of fiction, the author really had taken a raft journey with a number of her classmates during her college years. See "A

Conversation with Lee Smith" at the end of the novel, especially pages 387–89, for Smith's description of the actual raft trip that she took in 1966 with fifteen of her classmates from Hollins College, an all-women's college in Roanoke, Virginia.

2. Steven Mintz, *Huck's Raft: A History of American Childhood* (Cambridge, MA: Belknap Press, 2004).

3. Bob, the one-legged slave, claimed to own the wood-flat that he had "ketched," but that was only because "his marster didn' know it" (*HF* 56). As river salvage, the wood-flat would have belonged to Bob's master—at least if he had known about it.

4. Martin J. Norris, *The Laws of Salvage* (Mount Kisco, NY: Baker, Voorhis, 1958), 223–24.

5. Mark Twain, *The Adventures of Tom Sawyer*, in *Mark Twain: Mississippi Writings* (Berkeley, CA: Library of America, 1982), 87. The raft is referred to again on page 101 as "the small raft." Subsequent page citations from this novel, which was first published in 1876, are identified parenthetically as "*TS*" and are from this edition.

6. Charles Edward Russell, *A-Rafting on the Mississip'* (New York: Century, 1928), 81.

7. Walter A. Blair, *A Raft Pilot's Log: A History of the Great Rafting Industry on the Upper Mississippi, 1840–1915* (Cleveland, OH: Arthur H. Clark, 1930), 45. This Walter Blair is not to be confused with the Twain scholar of the same name who did so much to work out the complex history of the composition of *Huckleberry Finn*.

8. Robert F. Fries, *Empire in Pine: The Story of Lumbering in Wisconsin, 1830–1900*, rev. ed. (Madison: State Historical Society of Wisconsin, 1989), 32–33.

9. H. H. Bennett, *Story of a Raftsman's Life on the Wisconsin River* (Grand Rapids, WI: Chisolm Bros., n.d.).

10. Several books and articles were very helpful for my description of the assembly of cribs. The most useful were W. H. Glover, "Lumber Rafting on the Wisconsin River," in *Wisconsin Magazine of History*, December 1941, 156–62; and Malcolm Rosholt, *The Wisconsin Logging Book, 1839–1939*, 2nd ed. (Rosholt, WI: Rosholt House, 1981), 195–205. See also William J. Fox, *A History of the Lumber Industry in the State of New York* (Washington, DC: US Government Printing Office, 1902), 19–20; Agnes M. Larson, *History of*

the White Pine Industry in Minnesota (Minneapolis: University of Minnesota Press, 1949), 91–93; Russell, *A-Rafting*, 81–82; Blair, *Raft Pilot's Log*, 28–29; and Fries, *Empire in Pine*, 66.

11. Fries, *Empire in Pine*, 67.

12. Blair, *Raft Pilot's Log*, 26–27.

13. Mrs. Oliver Howard, "Rafting on the Mississippi in Early Days of Mark Twain," *Twainian* 19 (January-February 1957): 3.

14. Glover, "Lumber Rafting," 161–65.

15. Russell, *A-Rafting*, 82n. For another reference to Huck and Jim's little raft as a crib, see Sherwood Cummings, "Mark Twain's Movable Farm and the Evasion," *American Literature* 63 (1991): 443.

16. Michael Patrick Hearn, *The Annotated Huckleberry Finn* (New York: W. W. Norton, 2001), 74.

17. Rasmussen, *Critical Companion*, 198.

18. SparkNotes, "SparkNote on *The Adventures of Huckleberry Finn*," 2002, http://www.sparknotes.com/lit/huckfinn/.

19. Quoted in Rosholt, *Wisconsin Logging Book*, 195.

20. Michael A. Powell, *Mark Twain: A Raftsmen Episode Variorum* (Eugene, OR: Pacific Rim University Press, 2014), 73.

21. US Forest Service. "Weights of Various Woods Grown in the United States," Technical Note Number 218, Forest Products Laboratory, Madison, WI, July 1931.

22. Christian Schultz Jr., "Flatboat Fleets in 1808," in *Before Mark Twain: A Sampler of Old, Old Times on the Mississippi*, ed. John Francis McDermott (Carbondale: Southern Illinois University Press, 1968), 16. See also Fries, *Empire in Pine*, 68.

23. Russell, *A-Rafting*, 83.

24. Glover, *Lumber Rafting*, 170.

25. The discovery in 1990 of Twain's manuscript of the first half of *Huckleberry Finn* has given us valuable access to Twain's revisions for the novel. The most important of those are discussed in the nearly two hundred pages of reference materials (*HF* 363–561) at the end of the Fischer and Salamo edition.

26. Bernard DeVoto, ed., "Introduction," in Mark Twain, *Adventures of Huckleberry Finn (Tom Sawyer's Companion)* (1942; repr., Norwalk, CT: Easton Press, 1994), lix.

Chapter Two

1. Blair, *Raft Pilot's Log*, 30. When there were heavy side winds, the rafts were forced to tie up at the edge of the river until the wind died down. Glover, "Lumber Rafting," 170.

2. Blair, *Raft Pilot's Log*, 29.

3. Fries, *Empire in Pine*, 67–68.

4. Rosholt, *Wisconsin Logging Book*, 195.

5. Glover, "Lumber Rafting," 160.

6. Thomas Hart Benton, "A Note by the Illustrator," in Mark Twain, *Adventures of Huckleberry Finn (Tom Sawyer's Companion)*, ed. Bernard DeVoto (1942; repr., Norwalk, CT: Easton Press, 1994), lxxii–lxxiii. Benton made an entirely different, and far less accurate, depiction of Huck and Jim's raft for the mural illustrating "A Social History of the State of Missouri: *Huckleberry Finn*," which appears on the north wall of the Missouri State Museum. It is no better than Kemble's imagery. It shows the raft as a log raft, a single steering oar used as a rudder, and the wigwam as a round-based, cone-shaped, canvas-covered, Plains Indian tepee rather than a structure made of raft planks. A reproduction of Benton's mural appears on the cover of the edition of *Huckleberry Finn* edited by Gerald Graff and James Phelan (Boston: Bedford/St. Martin's, 1995).

7. Claude R. Flory, "Huck, Sam, and the Small-Pox," *Mark Twain Journal* 12, no. 3 (Winter 1964–1965): 8.

8. William L. Andrews, "Mark Twain and James W. C. Pennington: Huckleberry Finn's Smallpox Lie," *Studies in American Fiction* 9 (1981): 105.

9. Blair, *Raft Pilot's Log*, 38–39.

Chapter Three

1. George Byron Merrick, *Old Times on the Upper Mississippi: The Recollections of a Steamboat Pilot from 1854 to 1863* (Cleveland, OH: Arthur H. Clark, 1909), 22–24.

2. Douglas Anderson, "Reading the Pictures in *Huckleberry Finn*," *Arizona Quarterly* 42 (1986): 105.

3. James Stuart, *Three Years in North America* (New York: J. & J. Harper, 1833), 2:168. It is possible that Twain had read Stuart's book. If he had, it might have reminded him of the different waters in the Mississippi and Ohio Rivers, as described by Stuart: "The turbidity of the Mississippi, and the

comparative clearness of the Ohio, are distinctly observable in the rivers when their waters meet" (2:179). Compare that to this passage in *Huckleberry Finn*: "And they talked about how Ohio water didn't like to mix with Mississippi water. Ed said if you take the Mississippi on a rise when the Ohio is low, you'll find a wide band of clear water all the way down the east side of the Mississippi for a hundred mile or more" (*HF* 113).

4. Charles Lyell, *A Second Visit to the United States of North America* (New York: Harper & Brothers, 1849), 2:45.

5. Louis C. Hunter, *Steamboats on the Western Rivers: An Economic and Technological History* (Cambridge, MA: Harvard University Press, 1949), 264.

6. T. B. Thorpe, "Remembrances of the Mississippi," *Harper's*, December 1855, 37–38.

7. Stuart, *Three Years*, 2:169.

8. Merrick, *Old Times*, 59–60.

9. Thomas Cooley, ed., footnote in Mark Twain, *Adventures of Huckleberry Finn* (New York: W. W. Norton, 1999), 57; Emory Elliott, ed., "Explanatory Notes," in Mark Twain, *Adventures of Huckleberry Finn* (Oxford, UK: Oxford University Press, 2008), 277; *HF* 457 (Fischer and Salamo edition).

10. Hunter, *Steamboats*, 266.

11. "The Upper Mississippi," *Harper's*, March 1858, 444.

12. "Up the Mississippi," *Emerson's Magazine and Putnam's Monthly*, October 1857, 456.

13. W. G. Mepham, "Explosion of the Steamer *Pennsylvania*" in *Before Mark Twain: A Sampler of Old, Old Times on the Mississippi*, ed. John Francis McDermott (Carbondale: Southern Illinois University Press, 1968), 179. In Mepham's account the wood-flat was fetched from a nearby wood yard after the explosion rather than having already been in tow when the explosion occurred.

14. Elliott, "Explanatory Notes," 278.

15. Most of what I say in this section comes from Kevin J. Crisman and Arthur B. Cohn, *When Horses Walked on Water: Horse-Powered Ferries in Nineteenth-Century America* (Washington, DC: Smithsonian Institution Press, 1998). I highly recommend this book, especially part 1. Part 2 concerns itself with the excavation of a horse ferry, built around 1830 and sunk in Burlington Bay in Lake Champlain (Vermont). The book has many useful drawings and photographs.

16. Quoted in ibid., 54.

17. Stuart, *Three Years*, 2:194–95.

18. Ibid., 2:202–3.

19. "Up the Mississippi," 456.

20. T. B. Thorpe, "Remembrances of the Mississippi," *Harper's*, December 1855, 29.

Chapter Four

1. Schultz, "Flatboat Fleets," 19. See Peter G. Beidler, "Christian Schultz's *Travels*: A New Source for *Huckleberry Finn*," *English Language Notes* 28 (1990): 51–61, for a suggestion that Schultz's 1810 book, *Travels on an Inland Voyage*, was probably known to Twain.

2. Emerson Bennett, *Mike Fink: A Legend of the Ohio* (Cincinnati, OH: U. P. James, 1852), 28.

3. Thorpe, "Remembrances," *Harper's*, 30.

4. Robert H. Hirst, "Note on the Text," in Mark Twain, *Adventures of Huckleberry Finn (Tom Sawyer's Comrade)*, ed. Walter Blair and Victor Fischer (Berkeley: University of California Press, 1985), 450.

5. Peter Schmidt, "The 'Raftsmen's Passage,' Huck's Crisis of Whiteness, and *Huckleberry Finn* in U.S. Literary History," *Arizona Quarterly* 59, no. 2 (Summer 2003): 35.

6. DeVoto, "Introduction," x–xi. The raft episode was also put into chapter 16 of the novel in Bernard DeVoto, *The Portable Mark Twain* (New York: Viking, 1946).

7. Kenneth S. Lynn, "Huck and Jim," *Yale Review* 47 (1958): 425–26. In his own edition of the novel, published by Harcourt, Brace, and World in 1961, Lynn restored the raft episode in chapter 16.

8. Peter G. Beidler, "The Raft Episode in *Huckleberry Finn*," *Modern Fiction Studies* 14 (1968): 11–20. In addition to including the two reasons I discuss in this chapter, this article analyzes the importance of Huck's blurting out the name of the dead baby in the haunted barrel as his own name (15–20).

9. William R. Manierre, "On Keeping the Raftsmen's Passage in *Huckleberry Finn*," *English Language Notes* 6 (1968): 121.

10. Hirst, "Note," 450.

11. Jay E. Gillette, "Mark Twain's Art vs. Samuel Clemens' Business: Why the 'Raftsmen' Episode Disappeared from *Adventures of Huckleberry Finn*,"

Australasian Journal of American Studies 5 (December 1986): 9–10. Gillette did not acknowledge the contributions of earlier scholars.

12. David E. E. Sloane, *Adventures of Huckleberry Finn: American Comic Vision* (Boston: Twayne, 1988), 67–70.

13. Victor A. Doyno, ed., "Textual Addendum," in Mark Twain, *Adventures of Huckleberry Finn* (New York: Ivy, 1996), 341.

14. Schmidt, "'Raftsmen's Passage,'" 36, 42. Elsewhere in this article (54n5) Schmidt takes issue with Lucinda H. MacKethan, "Huck Finn and the Slave Narratives: Lighting Out as Design," *Southern Review* 20 (1984): 261, who wrote, "If Mark Twain had left the raft scene in chapter 16 he would have damaged the chapter's unity and obscured its focus. As it now stands, without the raft scene, the chapter begins with Jim's and Huck's search for Cairo's lights and ends with the lights of the steamboat bearing down on the runaways." I would point out that the light Huck and Jim were watching for at the start of chapter 16 was not of Cairo but of a cabin or a wood yard that could provide them with information about Cairo (*HF* 106). Only later did they decide to watch for Cairo (*HF* 123). MacKethan makes her statement almost in passing, however. It is not a major part of her argument.

15. Hamlin Lewis Hill, "Introduction," in Mark Twain, *Adventures of Huckleberry Finn*. Facsimile of 1st ed. (San Francisco: Chandler, 1962), xii.

16. Jonathan Arac, *Huckleberry Finn as Idol and Target: The Functions of Criticism in Our Time* (Madison: University of Wisconsin Press, 1997), 140–42.

17. Powell, *Mark Twain*, 77–78.

18. Arac, *Huckleberry Finn*, 140.

19. R. Kent Rasmussen, ed., letter no. 100, in *Dear Mark Twain: Letters from His Readers* (Berkeley: University of California Press, 2013), 147.

20. Fischer and Salamo's source is a note dated February 1, 1929, in a document in the John Hay Library of Rare Books and Special Collections at Brown University, Providence, RI.

21. Mark Twain, *The Autobiography of Mark Twain*, ed. Charles Neider (New York: Washington Square Press, 1961), 270.

22. Lewis Leary, "Troubles with Mark Twain: Some Considerations on Consistency," *Studies in American Fiction* 2 (1974): 101–2.

23. For further discussion of Huck's identification with Charles William Allbright, see Beidler, "Raft Episode," 15–19.

Chapter Five

1. Ceylon Childs Lincoln, "Personal Experiences of a Wisconsin River Raftsman," in *Proceedings of the State Historical Society of Wisconsin at Its Fifty-Eighth Annual Meeting* (Madison: State Historical Society of Wisconsin, 1911), 181–89.

2. This note and the next two notes, apparently written by the editor of the proceedings, were published with the original article. "The following article is adapted from a paper on lumbering in the Wisconsin pinery, prepared for us by Mr. Lincoln. Ceylon Childs Lincoln was born April 18, 1850, at Naperville, Dupage County, Illinois. While still very young his family moved to Berlin, Wisconsin, and thence (in the spring of 1856) to Wautoma. During the first year of the War of Secession, the two eldest Lincoln brothers enlisted; and in the autumn of 1863, their juniors, Orange M. and Ceylon C., then aged respectively but thirteen and fourteen years, entered the Union army. Ceylon was a member of Company D, 35th Wisconsin volunteer infantry. All three of his brothers were lost in the service; he, the only survivor in his family, was mustered out Dec. 1, 1865. Returning to Wautoma, Mr. Lincoln began in 1867 to learn the trade of a printer, being employed on the Waushara *Argus*, edited by R. L. D. Potter. It was while working at this trade that he made the voyage on a raft, narrated in the accompanying paper. In 1870 Mr. Lincoln married Melinda J. Duncan of Richford, and began caring for a farm a mile from Wautoma. Later he was [a] blacksmith (1873–78) in several neighboring villages, bought and put in cultivation (1878–85) 120 acres of unbroken land, and afterwards (1885–87) kept the 'Lincoln Hotel' at Wautoma. One of the earliest settlers of Tomahawk (1887), he was in 1895 appointed to a janitorship in the State Capitol, being assigned to duty in the Museum of this Society. When the institution moved to its new building (1900), Mr. Lincoln was continued in this employment, and served as the Museum janitor until 1909. He then resigned, because of ill health, and now conducts a small farm in the town of Rutland, Dane County."

3. "When a dam extended across the river, it was necessary to leave a gap at one point in its crest, from which an incline or 'slide' was built down stream. It was often a dangerous operation to conduct a raft safely over such a slide, for at the bottom it would duck under water, and the men be washed off. To prevent this, an apron was sometimes constructed at the foot of the slide, comprised of logs fastened to its lower edge, whose other ends floated free."

4. "Ellis, in *Wis. Hist. Colls.*, iii, p. 442, explains this term as follows: 'This footing it up over the falls after a piece is run down, is called by the men "gigging back"; it is generally done at a quick pace, and the distance traveled, from sun to sun, by a gang in running a rapid and "gigging back," is often fifty, sixty, or seventy miles a day, and forms a pretty severe introduction to the green-horns into the mysteries of going down on a raft.'"

Glossary of Nautical, Lumbering, and Other Technical Terms

Because modern readers may be unfamiliar with some of the terms used in this book, I provide here brief definitions and explanations.

binder planks. The heavy planks (also called **witch planks**) at the top of a crib, drilled to receive the grub stake and the witch.

birchbark canoe. A light vessel made by attaching birchbark to a slender frame.

boiler. The steam chamber on a steamboat.

bow. The front of a boat (rhymes with *now*, not *know*).

broadhorn. Another name for a **flatboat**—a large flat-bottomed barge, typically about a hundred feet long and thirty wide.

canoe. A long, narrow, and often tippy vessel propelled by a paddle. *See* **birchbark canoe**, **drift canoe,** and **dugout canoe.**

channel. The place in the river where the main current runs and where the water is usually the deepest.

cheats. Dishonest suppliers of firewood who shorted a woodpile or mixed in twisted or rotten wood.

checking (also called **snubbing**). Stopping a raft.

chute. A channel between an island and the shore, narrower than the main body of the river on the other side of the island.

cord. A stack of firewood four feet high by four feet wide by eight feet long (128 cubic feet).

cordwood. Firewood cut and stacked, ready to sell.

crib. A section of a lumber raft which, joined to other cribs, formed a **rapids piece,** a **Wisconsin raft,** or a **Mississippi raft.**

crossing. A place, usually at a curve in the river, where raftsmen had to maneuver themselves away from a likely collision with the riverbank and steer the raft back to the main channel.

cylinder-head. The cap on the cylinder on a steam engine. Its purpose was to contain the pressure so that the steam could drive the piston up or down.

dam. An obstruction in a river or stream, usually man-made, that raised the water level and impeded traffic.

drift canoe. An empty canoe that has not been properly secured and so floats off.

driftwood. Branches, bushes, and bark floating down a river.

double-hull ferry. A ferry boat that for increased stability, deck space, and minimal depth or draw, was built on two hulls.

dugout canoe. A heavy canoe made by chopping, burning, or scraping the excess wood out of a log so that it floats.

ferry. A boat designed for short and repetitive runs across a body of water.

flat. Shortened form of **flatboat.**

flatboat. A large flat-bottomed barge that could serve multiple purposes: to haul trade goods, people, livestock, farm crops, whatever. When used to haul cordwood it was referred to as a **wood-flat** or a **woodboat.** Depending on its function, it could be wholly or partially roofed in.

fleet. A number of rapids pieces fastened together.

flood trash. A raft that got trapped upstream by low water and had to wait until the next year to make a downriver run. Such rafts were waterlogged, heavy, low in the water, slow, and easily run aground.

foot of an island. The downstream end.

foundation planks. The heavy planks (also known as **grub planks**) at the bottom of a crib, drilled to receive the wide (that is, the lower) end of a **grub stake.**

furnace. The part of the engine in a steamship that contains the fire that heats the water to make steam. It was often referred to as a boiler, though that term usually referred to the steam chamber.

gig. To walk back upstream after running a slide or rapids so as to help bring another string of cribs down.

grub stakes (also known as **grub pins** or **grubs**). Short saplings trimmed to two-inch diameters and cut to lengths of about three or four feet, used to hold lumber cribs together.

guards. The guardrails on a steamboat.

gunwale. The upper edge or rim of a boat or canoe.

handspike. A long bar or pole with a steel spike and hook at one end used to pry loose cribs that are hung up on a sandbar.

headblock. A chunk of wood used to raise or lower the steering oar on the pivot pin to adjust the depth to which a steering oar was dipped into the water.

head of an island. The upstream end.

horse ferry. A boat powered by horses walking around a vertical shaft or on a horizontal treadmill.

hull. The part of a boat that is in contact with the water.

keel. A horizontal timber at the bottom center of a boat to keep it from drifting sideways in the water.

keelboat. A boat with curved sides rising above a keel.

landing. A place along a riverbank where boats could tie up, usually alongside a dock or wharf. Some had names, such as Booth's Landing.

lath. Lumber cut in thin strips to be used as backing for plaster.

log raft. A raft made of logs fastened together to be floated to a downriver sawmill.

lumber. Trees cut at a sawmill into planks and beams.

lumber raft. A raft made of stacked lumber fastened together to be floated to a downriver market.

Mississippi raft. A lumber raft made up of several Wisconsin rafts joined together to make their way together down the wide Mississippi River.

oar. A long navigational tool with a flat, tapered end, usually part of a matched pair, used to propel a small boat (such as a skiff). *See* **steering oar** and **paddle.**

oar pin. *See* **pivot pin.**

paddle. A short navigational tool with a flattened end, held with both hands, used to propel and steer a canoe.

pat Juba. Slap thighs and clap hands during a "break-down"—that is, during a fast-paced African American dance.

pilot. The person in charge of navigating a raft or steamboat.

Pinus strobus. White pine.

pirate. A person (sometimes called a **cheat**) who attempted to swindle
steamboat owners and crews by selling defective or mis-stacked firewood.

pivot pin. A vertical pin (also called an **oar pin**) that served as a kind of
oarlock for a steering oar, keeping it vertical and balanced. Often it was the
exposed part of a grub stake.

push-pole. A pole used to maneuver a raft in shallow water.

quartering. Compensating for the force of the current by aiming upstream of
one's actual destination.

rapids piece. Six or seven cribs fastened end-to-end in a line for running
rapids (sometimes called a **string**).

reef. A riverbank or shoal.

rise. The gradual increase in the level of a river caused by upriver precipitation
or melting.

rudder. A vertical steering board or paddle used at the rear of a boat that
moved under its own power. It would have been useless in steering a floating
raft drifting with the current. A steering oar was *not* a rudder, though it
could be used as one if a boat had its own source of power.

saddlebag. To hit an object in such a way that part goes on one side of the
object hit, part on the other side.

sawlogs. Trees cut to length with the branches removed, ready for the
sawmill.

scow. Another term for a **flat-boat**.

shingle. Short, thin-sliced, tapered piece of lumber used for roofing or siding.

skiff. A small boat made of overlapping planks and pointed on at least one
end, and powered by a rower with two oars, one on either side.

slide. A man-made slanting channel built into a river dam to permit rafts to
make their descent down the river.

starboard. The right ("stabboard") side of a raft or vessel.

steamboat. A large boat powered by a steam engine used to transport
passengers and freight.

steering oar. A long oar (also called a **sweep**), pivoting on a vertical pin, used
to steer a raft, avoid collisions with other rivercraft, and keep it in the main
channel.

stern oar. A steering oar at the back (aft) of a raft.

string. *See* **rapids piece**.

sucker. An inexperienced raftsman, especially one on his first journey (also, a native of Illinois).

sucker line. A safety line that raftsmen could take hold of when descending dangerous rapids or slides.

sweep. *See* **steering oar.**

teamboat. A boat powered by a team of horses.

thwart. A board fastened under the gunwales of a skiff to strengthen the structure and provide seating for passengers and rowers.

trading scow. A flatboat, often used for human habitation as well as hauling trade goods. A scow could be used as a wood-flat.

trotline. A strong fishing line with hooks fastened along it and laid on the bottom of a river, often at night, to catch catfish.

warping. The slow process of hauling a keelboat back upriver after it drifted to its destination (typically St. Louis or New Orleans). Warping usually involved the use of long poles pushing against the river bottom as laborers walked along the deck.

wharf. A large landing stage or dock on a riverbank to allow ships to tie up to load or discharge passengers and freight.

wharf boat. A boat used as a floating wharf. It could be let out or brought in as the river rose or fell.

wigwam. Originally a Native American structure, but also a term for a temporary structure built on rafts to afford protection from the elements.

Wisconsin raft. A lumber raft made up of several rapids pieces fastened side-by-side.

witch. A wedge device used, in conjunction with the protruding grub stakes, to pull the crib tight and hold the planks in place so they would not come loose and float away. The term is probably a result of linguistic drift from the word "wedge."

woodboat. *See* **wood-flat.**

wood-flat. A flatboat (often called a **woodboat**) that was loaded with firewood, ready to be sold to an upriver steamboat. It would be tied to the steamboat and unloaded as the steamboat continued on its journey, then cast off to drift back to the wood yard, where it was loaded up again in readiness for the next upriver steamboat. Towing the wood-flats during loading made sense to steamboat owners because they could continue their journey with minimal delay. It made sense to wood yard owners because it left room for other steamboats.

wood rank. A long, high stack of firewood ready for sale as fuel to a passing steamboat. Sometimes the term was used to indicate a twenty-cord stack of wood, but sometimes it was used less precisely as a synonym for wood pile.

wood yard. A place that sold stacked firewood (cordwood) as fuel to passing steamboats.

yawl. A boat, usually powered by two rowers, used to take passengers and freight to and from a vessel that was too large to tie up at the dock.

yokes. Short pieces of wood pre-drilled with two-inch holes to fit down over grub stakes to hold cribs together side-by-side.

Bibliography

Anderson, Douglas. "Reading the Pictures in *Huckleberry Finn*." *Arizona Quarterly* 42 (1986): 102–20.

Andrews, William L. "Mark Twain and James W. C. Pennington: Huckleberry Finn's Smallpox Lie." *Studies in American Fiction* 9 (1981): 103–12.

Arac, Jonathan. *Huckleberry Finn as Idol and Target: The Function of Criticism in Our Time.* Madison: University of Wisconsin Press, 1997.

Beidler, Peter G. "Christian Schultz's *Travels*: A New Source for *Huckleberry Finn?*" *English Language Notes* 28 (1990): 51–61.

———. "The Raft Episode in *Huckleberry Finn*." *Modern Fiction Studies* 14 (1968): 11–20.

Bennett, Emerson. *Mike Fink: A Legend of the Ohio.* Cincinnati, OH: U. P. James, 1852.

Bennett, H. H. *Story of a Raftsman's Life on the Wisconsin River.* Grand Rapids, WI: Chisolm Bros., n.d.

Benton, Thomas Hart. "A Note by the Illustrator." In Mark Twain, *Adventures of Huckleberry Finn (Tom Sawyer's Companion)*, edited by Bernard DeVoto, lxxi–lxxvi. 1942. Reprint, Norwalk, CT: Easton Press, 1994.

Blair, Walter A. *A Raft Pilot's Log: A History of the Great Rafting Industry on the Upper Mississippi, 1840–1915.* Cleveland, OH: Arthur H. Clark, 1930.

Carkeet, David. "The Dialects in *Huckleberry Finn*." *American Literature* 51 (1979): 315–32.

Crisman, Kevin J., and Arthur B. Cohn. *When Horses Walked on Water: Horse-Powered Ferries in Nineteenth-Century America.* Washington, DC: Smithsonian Institution Press, 1998.

Cummings, Sherwood. "Mark Twain's Movable Farm and the Evasion." *American Literature* 63 (1991): 440–58.

DeVoto, Bernard, ed. "Introduction." In Mark Twain, *Adventures of Huckleberry Finn (Tom Sawyer's Companion)*, ix–lxx. 1942. Reprint, Norwalk, CT: Easton Press, 1994.

———. *The Portable Mark Twain*. New York: Viking Press, 1946.

Doyno, Victor A., ed. "Textual Addendum." In Mark Twain, *Adventures of Huckleberry Finn*, 325–55. New York: Ivy, 1996.

Drake, Samuel Adams. *The Making of the Great West, 1512–1883*. New York: Charles Scribner's Sons, 1891.

Elliott, Emory, ed. "Explanatory Notes." In Mark Twain, *Adventures of Huckleberry Finn*, 275–84. Oxford, UK: Oxford University Press, 2008.

Flory, Claude R. "Huck, Sam, and the Small-Pox." *Mark Twain Journal* 12, no. 3 (Winter 1964–1965): 1–2, 8.

Fox, William J. *A History of the Lumber Industry in the State of New York*. Washington, DC: US Government Printing Office, 1902.

Fries, Robert F. *Empire in Pine: The Story of Lumbering in Wisconsin, 1830–1900*. Rev. ed. Madison: State Historical Society of Wisconsin, 1989.

Gillette, Jay E. "Mark Twain's Art vs. Samuel Clemens' Business: Why the 'Raftsmen' Episode Disappeared from *Adventures of Huckleberry Finn*." *Australasian Journal of American Studies* 5 (December 1986): 3–13.

Glover, W. H. "Lumber Rafting on the Wisconsin River." *Wisconsin Magazine of History*, December 1941, 155–77.

Hearn, Michael Patrick. *The Annotated Huckleberry Finn*. New York: W. W. Norton, 2001.

Hill, Hamlin Lewis. "Introduction." In Mark Twain, *Adventures of Huckleberry Finn*, vii–xvii. Facsimile of 1st ed. San Francisco: Chandler, 1962.

Hirst, Robert H. "Note on the Text." In Mark Twain, *Adventures of Huckleberry Finn (Tom Sawyer's Comrade)*, edited by Walter Blair and Victor Fischer, 447–51. Berkeley: University of California Press, 1985.

Howard, Mrs. Oliver. "Rafting on the Mississippi in Early Days of Mark Twain." *Twainian* 19 (January-February 1957: 3–4.

Hunter, Louis C. *Steamboats on the Western Rivers: An Economic and Technological History*. Cambridge, MA: Harvard University Press, 1949.

Larson, Agnes M. *History of the White Pine Industry in Minnesota*. Minneapolis: University of Minnesota Press, 1949.

Leary, Lewis. "Troubles with Mark Twain: Some Considerations on Consistency." *Studies in American Fiction* 2 (1974): 89–103.

Levy, Andrew. *Huck Finn's America: Mark Twain and the Era That Shaped His Masterpiece.* New York: Simon and Schuster, 2015.

Lincoln, Ceylon Childs. "Personal Experiences of a Wisconsin River Raftsman." In *Proceedings of the State Historical Society of Wisconsin at Its Fifty-Eighth Annual Meeting,* 181–89. Madison: State Historical Society of Wisconsin, 1911.

Lyell, Charles. *A Second Visit to the United States of North America.* 2 vols. New York: Harper & Brothers, 1849.

Lynn, Kenneth S. "Huck and Jim." *Yale Review* 47 (1958): 421–31.

MacKethan, Lucinda H. "Huck Finn and the Slave Narratives: Lighting Out as Design." *Southern Review* 20 (1984): 247–64.

Manierre, William R. "On Keeping the Raftsmen's Passage in *Huckleberry Finn.*" *English Language Notes* 6 (1968): 118–22.

McDermott, John Francis, ed. *Before Mark Twain: A Sampler of Old, Old Times on the Mississippi.* Carbondale: Southern Illinois University Press, 1968.

Mepham, W. G. "Explosion of the Steamer *Pennsylvania.*" In *Before Mark Twain: A Sampler of Old, Old Times on the Mississippi,* edited by John Francis McDermott, 178–86. Carbondale: Southern Illinois University Press, 1968.

Merrick, George Byron. *Old Times on the Upper Mississippi: The Recollections of a Steamboat Pilot from 1854 to 1863.* Cleveland, OH: Arthur H. Clark, 1909.

Mintz, Steven. *Huck's Raft: A History of American Childhood.* Cambridge, MA: Belknap Press, 2004.

Norris, Martin J. *The Laws of Salvage.* Mount Kisco, NY: Baker, Vooris, 1958.

Powell, Michael A. *Mark Twain: A Raftsmen Episode Variorum.* Eugene, OR: Pacific Rim University Press, 2014.

Rasmussen, R. Kent. *Critical Companion to Mark Twain: A Literary Reference to His Life and Work.* New York: Facts on File, 2007.

———, ed. *Dear Mark Twain: Letters from His Readers.* Berkeley: University of California Press, 2013.

Rosholt, Malcolm. *The Wisconsin Logging Book, 1839–1939.* 2nd ed. Rosholt, WI: Rosholt House, 1981.

Russell, Charles Edward. *A-Rafting on the Mississip'.* New York: Century, 1928.

Schmidt, Peter. "The 'Raftsmen's Passage,' Huck's Crisis of Whiteness, and *Huckleberry Finn* in U.S. Literary History." *Arizona Quarterly* 59, no. 2 (Summer 2003): 35–58.

Schultz, Christian Jr. "Flatboat Fleets in 1808." In *Before Mark Twain: A Sampler of Old, Old Times on the Mississippi*, edited by John Francis McDermott, 13–19. Carbondale: Southern Illinois University Press, 1968.

Sloane, David E. E. *Adventures of Huckleberry Finn: American Comic Vision.* Boston: Twayne, 1988.

Smith, Lee. *The Last Girls: A Novel.* New York: Ballantine Books, 2002.

Stuart, James. *Three Years in North America.* 2 vols. New York: J. & J. Harper, 1833.

Thorpe, T. B. "Remembrances of the Mississippi." *Harper's*, December 1855, 25–41.

Twain, Mark. *Adventures of Huckleberry Finn.* 1885. Edited by Sculley Bradley, Richard Croom Beatty, and E. Hudson Long. New York: W. W. Norton, 1961.

———. *Adventures of Huckleberry Finn.* Edited by Thomas Cooley. New York: W. W. Norton, 1999.

———. *Adventures of Huckleberry Finn (Tom Sawyer's Comrade).* Edited by Victor Fischer and Lin Salamo. Berkeley: University of California Press, 2001.

———. *Adventures of Huckleberry Finn.* Edited by Kenneth S. Lynn. New York: Harcourt, Brace & World, 1961.

———. *Adventures of Huckleberry Finn.* Edited by Robert G. O'Meally. New York: Barnes and Noble, 2003.

———. *The Adventures of Tom Sawyer.* 1876. In *Mark Twain: Mississippi Writings*, 1–215. Berkeley, CA: Library of America, 1982.

———. *The Autobiography of Mark Twain.* Edited by Charles Neider. New York: Washington Square Press, 1961.

———. *Life on the Mississippi.* 1883. In *Mark Twain: Mississippi Writings*, 217–616. Berkeley, CA: Library of America, 1982.

"The Upper Mississippi." *Harper's*, March 1858, 433–54.

"Up the Mississippi." *Emerson's Magazine and Putnam's Monthly*, October 1857, 433–56.

US Forest Service. "Weights of Various Woods Grown in the United States." Technical Note Number 218, Forest Products Laboratory, Madison, WI, July 1931.

Index

Note: numbers in bold refer to illustrations.